THE END OF THE PROFESSIONS?

Professions and professional activity are undergoing dramatic changes as we approach the millennium. This interdisciplinary volume presents an overview of conceptual issues and considers the practical issues facing professionals today. It has two key objectives:

- to understand the nature of the changes in professional activity;
- to see this restructuring in the context of wider socio-economic processes.

Examining the professional areas of medicine, education, law and accountancy, the authors illustrate how the nature of professional activity is changing: decision-making power is being shifted away from the holders of specialised knowledge and towards clients and managers. Although this might seem to signify an end to traditional notions of professionalism involving trust, responsibility and self-organisation, they argue that this does not necessarily mean an end to professionalism itself, but rather a restructuring of its significance and functioning.

This process is of central importance to political economists, sociologists, organisation and management theorists, and anyone who is trying to understand the significance of professional organisation in modern-day British society.

Jane Broadbent is Reader in Accounting at the University of Essex. She is the author of many articles on accounting and accountability, particularly in the public sector.

Michael Dietrich lectures at the University of Sheffield. He writes widely on the economics of the firm and organisation, his work includes *Transaction Cost Economics and Beyond*.

Jennifer Roberts lectures at the University of Sheffield. She writes in the areas of feminisation, professionalisation and labour economics.

ROUTLEDGE STUDIES IN BUSINESS ORGANIZATION AND NETWORKS

THE END OF
THE PROFESSIONS?

The restructuring of professional work

Edited by
Jane Broadbent, Michael Dietrich and
Jennifer Roberts

Routledge
Taylor & Francis Group

LONDON AND NEW YORK

First published 1997
by Routledge
2 Park Square, Milton Park, Abingdon, Oxon OX14 4RN

Reprinted 1999

Simultaneously published in the USA and Canada
by Routledge

Transferred to Digital Printing 2006

Routledge is an imprint of the Taylor & Francis Group

First issued in paperback 2016

Typeset in Palatino by
Ponting–Green Publishing Services, Chesham,
Buckinghamshire

British Library Cataloguing in Publication Data
A catalogue record for this book is available from
the British Library

Library of Congress Cataloging in Publication Data
The End of the Professions? The restructuring of professional
work / edited by Jane Broadbent, Michael Dietrich, and
Jennifer Roberts
p.   cm.
Includes bibliographical references and index.
1. Professional corporations–Management
2. Corporate reorganizations.
I. Broadbent, Pamela Jane.   II. Dietrich, Michael.
III. Roberts, Jennifer.
HD62.65.E53   1997
658–dc20   96–19119

ISBN13: 978-0-415-14300-4 (hbk)
ISBN13: 978-1-138-96877-6 (pbk)

Publisher's Note
The publisher has gone to great lengths to ensure
the quality of this reprint but points out that some
imperfections in the original may be apparent

CONTENTS

v

PREFACE

This book emerged from a workshop held at the University of Sheffield under the auspices of Sheffield University Management School and the Political Economy Research Centre (PERC). A number of us at the University realised that work on professionalism was being undertaken without the benefit of interdepartmental cross-fertilisation; we were attempting to understand how and why professionalism is changing in a context of a single discipline or single professional orientation. Such was the enthusiasm generated at the workshop that it was decided to build on the work already undertaken. Hence the organisers became editors and Routledge were sufficiently impressed with the project to offer us a contract.

Five of the nine chapters in this volume first appeared as papers at the Sheffield University workshop, i.e. chapters 2, 3, 5, 6 and 7. Chapters 4 and 8 were selected from a number offered after the workshop by people who felt they had a particular contribution to make. David Marquand was typically generous in his willingness to write chapter 9. The authors have written chapter 1 with the intention of offering not only an introduction to the volume but a contribution in its own right. The chapters taken as a whole offer a discussion of modern professionalism that is theoretical and applied and written by, and relevant for, academics as well as practitioners.

This volume, as well as being a project in its own right, is part of a wider political economy project being undertaken by PERC at the University of Sheffield. Both this work and PERC are based on the belief that the perspectives of the past cannot address the problems posed by recent economic and political transformations. The aim is, therefore, to explore new issues in political economy from an interdisciplinary standpoint. This volume is a concrete example of this work being undertaken at Sheffield.

Last, but not least, the editors would like to thank the many people who have made the production of this volume a much easier task than it might otherwise have been. In particular Jane Mallinson provided administrative support. Sean Holly and Anthony Fretwell-Downing were happy to offer financial assistance that contributed to the success of the workshop. Finally, the people who attended the workshop, all of whom contributed in some way, can be thanked for collectively energising the authors. Readers can decide if all our efforts are worthwhile.

Jane Broadbent
Michael Dietrich
Jennifer Roberts

CONTRIBUTORS

Jane Broadbent is Reader in Accounting at the University of Essex.

Michael Dietrich is Lecturer in Economics at the University of Sheffield.

Rosalind Eve works for the Framework for Appropriate Care Throughout Sheffield at the University of Sheffield Centre for Health and Related Research.

Gerard Hanlon is Lecturer in Organisational Theory at the Management Centre, King's College, London.

Paul Hodgkin works for the Framework for Appropriate Care Throughout Sheffield at the University of Sheffield Centre for Health and Related Research.

Tom Kennie is Director of PMD Consulting and part-time Professor at Sheffield Hallam University.

Richard Laughlin is Professor of Accounting at the University of Essex.

David Marquand is Principal of Mansfield College, Oxford and Chair of the Advisory Board of the Political Economy Research Centre at the University of Sheffield.

Robin Middlehurst is Director of the Quality Enhancement Group at the Higher Education Quality Council.

Jon Nixon is Professor of Education at Canterbury Christ Church College at the University of Kent.

Jennifer Roberts is Lecturer in Economics at the University of Sheffield.

Joanna Shapland is Professor of Law and Director of the Institute for the Study of the Legal Profession at the University of Sheffield.

1

THE END OF THE PROFESSIONS?

Jane Broadbent, Michael Dietrich and Jennifer Roberts

INTRODUCTION

Readers of this volume are likely to have a fairly well developed understanding of what it means to be a professional or to behave professionally, an understanding that will have been developed by an extended period of formal or informal training and enculturation as well as day-to-day practice in our working lives. It follows that, perhaps, readers may also have been attracted to this volume because they are aware of the ways in which their perceived professional status is being degraded. In many areas, as discussed in the chapters presented here, institutionalised control is being degraded by the introduction of systems of individual accountability based on customer reaction. We are all facing and coping with differing degrees of success, the stresses and contradictions of changing work and organisational practices. To many of us this may seem like an end to professionalism as we perceive it. The norms and routines that have served us well are being cast as outdated practices unsuited to a new era and we are in the course of developing new understandings of what is meant by the term professionalism.

But we must be careful not to jump to conclusions about the nature of the processes which affect us: an individual or collective response to an uncertain future is not the same as understanding the dynamics of change. It is a myth to presume that common sense or an intuitive understanding is sufficient to lead us through the messiness and uncertainties of a changing world. We all have particular mental pictures and common senses of professional practice that have been developed in particular contexts. Our reactions to an uncertain future will be conditioned by this deadweight of accumulated practice. But without a more general understanding of the shifting landscape that charts the movement from where we have come from to where we are going, our responses are likely to be partial at best. To this extent the chapters presented here have a very practical purpose: to help us grapple with changing professional practice.

This greater understanding of the dynamics of change will give an additional benefit. We will see that professionalism is not at an end. To

1

this extent the question mark in the title of this volume is not simply a marketing device, it is meant to reflect the differences between what we might be experiencing in our everyday lives and the significance of these experiences in a more general context. This wider context is presented in both the theoretical and applied chapters of this volume. They suggest four broad features on the restructuring of professional work:

1 There is a fundamental rationale for professionalism, hence professional organisation cannot simply be curtailed or ended as if it was an optional extra to the way in which we choose to institutionalise our socio-economic practices. This set of common roots allows us to talk of professionalism as a single set of institutionalised practices. Obviously these practices may blur at the edges (for instance we might debate whether the activities of social work or marketing comprise professional activity), but we can be guided by the epistemological principle that the exceptions prove the rule.

2 We should not oversimplify the nature of professionalism, rather it is a diverse set of practices. This diversity is based on two factors. First, different professions have to grapple with particular conditions that are not common; to put it bluntly nurses, accountants and architects have particular jobs to do. Second, much professional practice, in all spheres, is based on informal norms as well as explicit rules. These norms are embedded in wider social practices and hence reflect the ways in which we differ by class, sex, race, region, age, parental status to name but a few factors. It follows that, for example, different teachers might perceive the nature of professionalism, in all its subtle detail, in different ways.

3 If we recognise both the common roots and the (sometimes subtle) diversity of professionalism we are in a good position to understand the current era of change. Inevitably this change is contradictory in terms of the new practices involved (this is why it is stressful and uncertain) because it brings to the surface the differences in existing relationships. The informal becomes apparent because of the way in which it clashes with an emerging set of practices.

4 Finally, we should be aware of the dynamism of the current era. The way in which the fundamental rationale for professionalism works itself out in practice depends on particular historical conditions. It follows that there is no single, ahistorical set of professional practices. At the same time, however, we should guard against viewing historical change as simply happening in a linear manner. A shift from one set of institutional practices to another requires change agents, without which extinction will occur. Hence the changes we are experiencing may be initial responses to environmental shifts and reactions to these shifts. This fluid situation should not be confused with reinstitutionalised

practices. What finally emerges may be very different, but the current disturbance may be viewed (in retrospect) as necessary.

These four features reappear in each of the eight remaining chapters of this volume. Obviously the particular emphasis of the theoretical or applied subject matter leads to orientation in a particular direction, but we should be aware that there is a wood among the trees. Before summarising the arguments presented in each of these chapters, this introduction will explore the nature of the wood in more detail. In particular the general nature of the changes will be examined.

THE DEVELOPMENT OF THE PROFESSIONS

Following Middlehurst and Kennie in chapter 4 of this volume, we can trace back many centuries the early development of professions, and in particular medicine, law and divinity. One notable contextual factor, which may be seen to have some relevance in this respect, is early links with the established church facilitating autonomy and social status which have become key factors in the identification of professional activity. The modern status of professionals is perhaps based more firmly in the nineteenth century where the links to the church are perhaps echoed in the sense of 'Victorian' responsibility with the rigid social hierarchies this involves. Clearly this fertile breeding ground for the early professions produced a strong emphasis on social status. Professional status was rooted in the notion of the 'gentlemanly conduct' of those who were members of the group. This was seen to be a guarantee of the integrity of the professional providing services to a public who were not knowledge-able purchasers. Indeed, some work on the early professional history of the accounting profession suggests that broader moral lapses as much as lapses in professional competence were at the root of the generation of a code of discipline (Walker, 1996). In general, institutional, scientific and social developments had direct impacts on key professions: for example, law, accounting, medicine, engineers, chemists. These ideas of professions still linger in our collective consciousness, but we should be aware of the ways in which they have been channelled by the twentieth century.

As we have implied above, the evolution of professionalism in the twentieth century cannot be understood without reference to key develop-ments in the societal contextual tapestry that have occurred and which form a backdrop for the particular changes. One such contextual factor which has perhaps affected professional development is the advent of 'scientific management' or Taylorism (and associated organisational and economic practices and developments). This was based on a philosophy of separating conception and execution of tasks, that is to say dif-ferentiating 'thinking' from 'doing'. This is called a philosophy rather than

3

a set of practices for two reasons. First, there was an almost universal defence from the 'doers' from the developing trade union movement, as well as a scepticism from some of the employers who worried about labour unrest, hence the control which Taylorism sought to impose was always contested. Second, it was never a universal practice: for example, it was highly appropriate in car manufacture, but largely inappropriate in machine tools manufacture. The basic difference between the two situations is that in one case the knowledge necessary for 'thinking' is separable from the 'doing' and in the other is not. Hence, whilst Taylorism as a set of specific practices was never universal it did inform a management philosophy: that managers had a right to manage. In the early years of this century this 'right to manage' only affected the craftspeople and the working classes. Arguably, scientific management both promoted and was promoted by a belief that there was a distinction to be made between conception and execution – thinking and doing. The implication for professionalism was that this allowed a 'scientific' rationale for professional status and autonomy in an era when Victorian ideas of social status were becoming largely obsolete. Professionals were 'thinkers' who were not subject to the managerial control which scientific management introduced. However, as the century has progressed, the ideology of the 'manager's right to manage' has been consolidated to such an extent that this prerogative is now seen as appropriate to extend to professional activities, the implications of which are discussed later in this chapter.

The philosophical or ideological underpinning of Taylorism was accompanied by another, contextual factor which was also important in developing professionalism: the development of the large scale organisation with characteristic mass production strategies. This might be seen to have influenced the need for more systematic control of the workforce (Braverman, 1974) but it also introduced the necessity of new specialist organisation tasks: financial management, marketing, research and development, etc. This is of interest for two reasons. First it gave some established professions, particularly accounting and law, a new relevance. Second, it illustrates the complex socio-economic context in which professional projects develop. This introduces the interesting question as to whether managers themselves can be classed as professionals, a subject that we will return to later in this chapter. In general there was no social recognition of their status in the early part of the century. For the moment we can point out that the necessary autonomy and tacit knowledge, which we see as defining characteristics of professionalism (along with training, internal control, etc.) were not necessarily present for line management, although in many cases the managers would have liked to have thought it was. An interesting question is whether this is still the case; at the same time we might also ask whether other new activities which arose from this new organisational structure (marketing for example) comprise profes-

4

sions? We will not offer an unambiguous answer here, but merely point out that this ambiguity is present in the very notion of professionalism.

A final contextual issue to be considered is the growth of the public sector and in this respect we can consider the way in which the Keynes-Beveridge consensus (as it is called in the UK) linking economic and social welfare reforms was implemented. In the development of the welfare state, institutions which took up the organisation of a number of professional services were born. In this process the professional status and autonomy of existing and developing professional groups was embedded in hierarchically organised welfare services. It was in these bureaucracies that a different notion of professionalism developed from that of the independent and ancient professions of, for example, law and medicine which had existed previously. The differences have resulted in a division between private and public sector professionalism that Perkin (1989, 1996) has consistently argued is central to the development of professions. In the public sector nominal hierarchical superiors were effectively impotent in terms of control of both detailed strategies and operations. The lack of direct control was suffered by both the suppliers of finance (i.e. the relevant level of the state) and users of services who were meant to gratefully accept the specialist activity supplied. The users of the services, the equivalent of Taylorist 'doers' in the private sector, had neither the equivalent of trade union power nor specialist knowledge to counter professional power. The post-war development of health services and school education in the UK where clinicians and teachers respectively controlled areas of their activity in a relatively autonomous way is illustrative here, as are the later developments in university education and social services. The case of medicine is particularly revealing (see chapter 5) as the new Health Ministry had to submit to the power of the British Medical Association in a way that ensured a continuing professional status. The implications of current reforms which have challenged this situation are equally revealing, as will be discussed shortly.

In summary, a brief overview of some of the currents from the first three-quarters of the twentieth century illustrates some of the ways in which professionalism can develop, although it should be recognised we have given a mere gloss over the complexities involved. One element of this development which we see as important and which has been presented here is the extent to which professionalism and Taylorism appear to be intwined. Early notions of scientific management provided no challenge to professionalism and indeed provided it with some legitimacy. More recently the ideas of Taylor have been seen as providing a template for approaches by which to control professional activity. However, these ideas have, since their inception, been under fairly constant attack. Economic criticisms emphasise the ways in which scientific management is demotivating and inappropriate in a dynamic and complex world.

5

Moral-ethical-political criticisms emphasise the undemocratic and in-human nature of its practices. This raises questions about the relevance of the transfer of this control approach to the professional sphere. This should not be taken to imply that we can ignore the issue. Professionalism was in earlier periods less subject to question and subject to the security of professional autonomy and the guiding role of strong professional ethics. More recently professional autonomy and ethical principles are frequently being cast as obsolete and irrelevant to the current era. But, a simple counter to such arguments based on the prerogative of what has happened in the past is difficult to sustain.

DEVELOPING THE NOTION OF PROFESSIONALISM

An examination of both the changing role of the professional and the control of professional activity is the central task of this volume. This recent impetus towards a changing professional role can be seen against the resurgence of neo-liberal ideas and practices. Neo-liberalism can be seen as a reaction to the post-war consensus. Marquand (1988), following the work of Reich in the USA, argues that there has been a move from the notion of a 'civic culture' of equitable consumption to a 'business culture' of profitable production. The movement should not be confused with a return to nineteenth century practices: this is mere rhetoric that has no real basis in reality. The central characteristics of the nineteenth century view on professionalism were, as we discussed earlier, seen to be an emphasis on two elements, social status and key institutional-scientific develop-ments. This is no longer the case, the first of these factors is lacking, arguably because of the implications of capitalist growth in the post-war 'golden era'. The second set of factors remains partially relevant, par-ticularly in terms of scientific development, but institutional evolution has more recently emphasised the supremacy of the individual over the social and ownership over responsibility. Contemporary neo-liberalism sees

> a government machine at the mercy of professional interests who ceaselessly seek to extract increased resources and to grant more power to sectional groups.
>
> (Miller and Rose, 1991: 129)

The thrust of neo-liberalism, thus, views professionals with antipathy. Neither is this distrust one sided. A neo-liberal emphasis on individuality and rights linked to ownership can be problematic for many professionals: particularly for those operating in the public sector: ideas of profession-alism often stress rights based on citizenship.

Professionals are seen as problematic for neo-liberals as their relative autonomy provides problems of control. For this reason the state has looked to demanding accountability for the activities of professionals in a manner which is sometimes reminiscent of the tenets of scientific management. Thus, the chapters which follow provide accounts of what is often seen to be attempts to produce a standardisation of professional activity in order to control it. This raises questions as to the potential for the development of professional activity. We will argue that the emphasis on individual-ownership which is currently prevalent might well be seen in retrospect as a transitional phase that provides a means of breaking previous professional practices and norms. The development of a new professionalism, we argue, requires a reinstitutionalised sense of social responsibility.

In exploring the development of professional practice, recognition must be given to the context in which those changes are located. The current era has been dominated by a number of changes; we highlight, in no order of importance, development of the realms of technological, organisational, socio-economic and state policies. These impinge upon professional development in a number of ways.

Technological change is being dominated by information and bio-technologies. These have a unique set of characteristics that are forcing socio-economic restructuring. In addition to providing obvious new markets and products that people want to buy they are generic inputs into other production processes. In short, new technologies are both pulling and pushing change. These changes are having a number of effects on professionals. Just as in the nineteenth century, new technologies are promoting the development of new experts, for example IT specialists, and this raises the question as to whether this body of people constitutes an emerging profession? The practice requires a body of specialist knowledge, along with a particular language and training requirements. The way this might develop is mere speculation. In addition to providing a possible impetus for new professional development, new technologies are disrupting existing professions. Information is now more mobile and available (but not completely so: see chapter 2) and this can undermine the role of specialists (see chapter 8 with regard to auditing). Furthermore, new technologies facilitate decentralisation accompanied by tighter accountability. This type of control (typical of neo-liberalism and providing accountability based on the standardisation of Taylorism) can undermine autonomy and is increasingly used in both the public and private sectors in the UK. In short, while new technologies might restructure professionalism we cannot predict a unique effect.

Organisational change is to some extent using this new technological capability but is also separate from it. Some important dimensions of the current emphasis can be explained in terms of flexible exploitation of core capabilities. The ideas of 'flexibility' and 'core capabilities' will be discussed in turn. Frequently, flexibility is presented in terms of an ability to 'hire and fire' labour, but in addition there is an alternative meaning, that we will argue is more important within the context of professionalism. The term also has a functional meaning: people must have the ability to do different tasks. This latter interpretation requires greater skills and training as well as a degree of on-the-job autonomy – professional characteristics. But the requirements for quantitative and functional flexibility are to some extent contradictory. It is difficult to motivate someone to retrain and to act in a responsible manner if job insecurity is high.

The management of this problem, in an uncertain world, has combined with the second idea, that of exploiting core capabilities. Firms are increasingly using subcontractors and specialists to provide goods and services that lie outside the core of production by motivated employees. This has had two important socio-economic effects. First, core workers and specialists are providing what are, in effect, professional services. This characterisation is based on a necessary degree of specialist knowledge and autonomy. The extent to which the defining characteristic of internal professional control is likely to be present is a debatable issue that will be discussed shortly. The second important socio-economic effect is the implications of subcontracting for dual labour markets. Ideas of professionalised labour are highly inappropriate for insecure, marginalised, temporary work.

The developments alluded to here seem to be to some extent a general characteristic of the current era. But in addition, in the UK as well as elsewhere, they have been stimulated by recent government policies that have explicitly deregulated labour markets, along with general policies of deregulation and privatisation. In terms of understanding the meaning of new professionalism these state sponsored developments are likely to have a number of effects. First, the emphasis of the policies has been on quantitative rather than functional flexibility; as pointed out earlier, the latter requires a reduction in hire and fire capabilities. Hence the logic of current policies would seem to lead to a deprofessionalisation of UK society. At the same time, however, this professionalisation is necessary (at least in part) to effectively exploit emerging markets, the implications of which will be developed in a moment. The second important effect of the current era, and state sponsored change, is a shift away from state economic influence towards company strategic autonomy. An important implication here is that control of labour is being internalised within organisations, the target being a reduction in trade union and state influence. But this corporatisation of decision making has implications for professionalism. We are moving away from action based on professional ethic towards action based on organisational strategy; witness, for example, the way in which public statements in the UK Health Service have to be channelled through official management structures with contractual limits on public statements now existing in nurse and doctor contracts. The implications of this second shift are complex to identify. We are seeing a change in ideas of professional practice. But equally, the logic of the developments requires a reprofessionalisation of tasks. We once again seem to have arrived at a potential inconsistency for the current era.

We are now in a position to discuss whether current changes indicate an end to professionalism or a restructuring of its form. In terms of organisational practice we seem to be seeing a move towards a new managerialism. But is this shift transitory or permanent? Or to put the same matter in a different way: are managers the new professionals? To understand the issues here we can make direct reference to some of the new managerial writing. Take, for example, the arguments of Drucker (1988). He suggests that we are seeing the emergence of a 'new organ-isation'. He compares this organisation with an orchestra. Detailed organisational tasks are undertaken by specialists, i.e. the equivalent of musicians. But, just as an orchestra needs a conductor to maintain musical coherence, an organisation needs a strategist to generate a sense of purpose and to maintain control.

Drucker's ideas are mentioned here because they seem to capture the spirit of the age. We should be careful, however, in how we interpret their substantive meaning. It was suggested earlier that Taylorism must be viewed as a philosophy rather than a set of universal practices. Similarly the 'new organisation' must be viewed in an equivalent way. It cannot be universal for at least two reasons. First, it ignores the important sectors of the economy based on insecure and part-time employment. Both in-security and non full-time working are inconsistent with unproblematic organisational commitment. Second, the vision of a 'new organisation' ignores the messiness of organisational politics and social interaction. This messiness is present in an orchestra but it is manageable because musician-ship, in general, is a profession. In other words different musicians have a remarkably close identity and ethic that simplifies orchestral functioning. The 'new organisation', however, is based on combining different know-ledge bases and perspectives but at the same time generating an organ-isational perspective.

It would seem to follow that the 'new organisation' is at best partial, and inherently contains tensions. It requires professional behaviour from specialists alongside a potential undermining of professional expertise because of the requirement of a single strategic vision. This character-isation will almost inevitably involve stress points as endemic aspects of organisational functioning. The only way that we can overcome these problems is to suggest that top management, i.e. the general strategists, are the only professionals. But this is clearly not tenable because it involves moving back to a Taylorist philosophy from which the new organisation is attempting to move.

If we are to reconcile the 'new organisation' with decentralised profes-sional behaviour we must characterise top management as change agents not professionals and not definers of the professional task. The management of change, if it is to be successful, would seem to require a respect for professional practice. But this new professionalism would seem to involve a number of tensions of which three would seem to be of key importance:

1 A need to accommodate professional autonomy compared to an organisational need to develop strategic control.
2 The development of a professional identity rather than simply the development of an organisational identity.
3 A respect for professional practice compared to the need to ensure change in that practice.

The picture painted here is that the new professionals are partially autonomous (point 1). Organisational functioning must be based on multiple identities (point 2) which strategists must accommodate. Finally, professional practice is not cast in stone (point 3). The tensions involved in these three points are potentially enormous. Professionals cannot be simply told what to do, whom to identify with, and how to change, which requires a significant shift in characteristic modern organisational functioning in the UK.

In short, this current organisational functioning would seem to be essentially transitional rather than an indicator of future characteristics. This may be a difficult conclusion for current strategists to accept, because apart from anything else it implies a diminution of their power and vision of the world. But at the same time it requires a shift in previous professional practice towards accepting organisational identity and change. The various chapters of this volume chart the various ways that these tensions are being managed, or not as the case may be. The collective picture painted by this work seems to indicate that there is no single way of managing the organisational dynamics summarised in the three points highlighted above. Rather organisational solutions respond to the characteristics of particular activities as well as the general socio-economic environment.

OUTLINE OF THE VOLUME

In addressing these issues the authors of the chapters provide their individual perspectives on the themes highlighted above, as well as on their own particular concerns. In providing a background and overview to the debates the first part of the book, chapters 1-4, turns to some conceptual issues. In chapter 2 Dietrich and Roberts address the thorny question as to whether there is any economic justification for the notion of professionalism, and they combine economic and sociological insights to provide a more complete understanding of the idea of professionalism. In doing this they provide a rich discussion of the justifications of profession-alism and a more dynamic analysis of professional development and decline. Turning next to the issue of professional power, in chapter 3 Broadbent and Laughlin discuss the ways in which attempts have been made to use accounting type controls to control professional activity. Their analysis is based particularly in the public sector and addresses the way that organisational changes in this sector have affected the role of profes-sionals working within this sphere. Their plea is for an evaluation of the changes which they see as possibly destructive of some of the key professional values in these organisations.

Chapter 4, by Middlehurst and Kennie, provides an exploration of professionalism by examining the evolution of professional activity de-veloped in the early part of this chapter. They seek to provide a framework for understanding the development of professional practice. It contrasts the differing context of those professionals in the private sector with those who are employed in the public sector. Recognising the need for change in the dynamic environment which exists for today's professional actors they develop a discussion on the issue of leadership. Their chapter concludes with a look towards the benefits of professionalism and the way in which it might be redefined and extended by an integration of the role of leadership and management.

The second part of the book, chapters 5–8, provides insights into the situations of professionals who are subject to the many changes which have been discussed earlier. Starting in chapter 5 with the case of medicine, Eve and Hodgkin provide a reflection from the point of view of two participants in the system. Their account illustrates the increased com-plexity of and the growing tensions between objectives of a system which are not mutually compatible. In this context they are clearly concerned with the extent to which the quality of medical care can be optimised, whilst recognising that some diversity of practice has to be accommodated and utilised to ensure an upward learning curve for the community as a whole. The authors clearly reject the notion of managerial control of the professional, nevertheless, they accept a need for some development of the notion of professionalism. In particular they argue for retaining profes-sional control, placing it in a context in which emphasis is put on the clarity of the constraints in which the system operates.

In his discussion of education in chapter 6, Nixon locates the roots of changes in the sector in the debates of Snow and Leavis and their disagreement over the relative importance of, on the one hand, science, technology and vocational education, and on the other, that of moral agency, judgement and responsibility. He argues that the earlier belief in the 'white heat of technology' provides a platform from which we can better understand the imperative to move from a liberal humanistic education system towards a mass system based on vocational imperatives.

11

The implications of this on the subjective experience of university lecturers and the effects on their practice are reflected in this chapter. The tensions between research and teaching and the fragmentation of occupations in the academic field are highlighted. Whilst recognising that challenges involve the development of different notions of professionalism in universities, Nixon argues cogently for a recognition of the values which historically have informed the development of the profession. This recognition should particularly be adopted in the areas of educational management and policy development.

Chapter 7, by Hanlon and Shapland, considers the fragmenting nature of the legal profession and in particular solicitors. They argue that the solicitors' profession is splitting into at least two quite separate segments. This division can be broadly described as depending on firm size, but underlying criteria for the fragmentation include client type, work performed, professional-client interaction and form of professional regulation. Small firms find themselves in an increasingly competitive, cost conscious market, providing a standardised service based largely on conveyancing and personal law to relatively powerless individual clients. In contrast large law firms are increasingly involved as business advisers to large, and powerful, corporations – an area in which the Big Six accounting firms are also present. This is resulting in increased tensions within the solicitors' profession, and Hanlon and Shapland argue that very different regulatory environments are required to control these distinct areas of law, and question the future of a single professional association in this context.

The shifting nature of the accountancy profession is considered in chapter 8. The ways in which the Big Six international firms have benefited from the 1980s is stressed. The increasing commercialisation of professionalism in this leading sector is leading to a downgrading of auditing and an emphasis placed on more profitable activities. In addition, the restructuring of the nature of professionalism in this sector has gone hand-in-hand with changes in the ways in which the large accounting firms are organised and managed; but Hanlon argues that professionalism is being commercialised not downgraded. In the final part of chapter 8 the changes in the accountancy sector are linked to wider socio-economic developments involving a shift from 'Fordism' towards 'flexible accumulation'.

Finally, in chapter 9, Marquand returns to general themes and examines the socio-political context within which future professionalism will be developing. In addition to being a contribution in its own right, the final chapter is a conclusion to the volume. The various themes set out in chapter 1, and developed in particular contexts in the intervening discussion, are brought together by Marquand. In particular, he examines how the problems and contradictions that face new professionals can be managed and reconciled in different ways. These differences depend not only on the particular characteristics of the professions but also on the general socio-political environment within which developments take place. It is this latter subject that is taken up in chapter 9. The ways in which the political landscape might evolve are analysed here and the implications for professions explored. A similar conclusion is drawn to that emphasised in all chapters: we are not seeing an end to professionalism, but we cannot simply extrapolate past practices to predict the forms of professional behaviour that will come to dominate in the twenty-first century.

REFERENCES

Braverman, H. (1974) *Labour and Monopoly Capital*, New York: Monthly Review Press.

Drucker, P.F. (1988) 'The coming of the new organisation', *Harvard Business Review*, January–February: 45–53.

Marquand, D. (1988) *The Unprincipled Society: New Demands and Old Politics*, London: Fontana Press.

Miller, P. and Rose, N. (1991) 'Programming the poor: Poverty, calculation and expertise', in J. Lehto (ed.) *Deprivation, Social Welfare and Expertise*, Helsinki: National Agency for Welfare and Health Research, Report 7: 117–40.

Perkin, H. (1989) *The Rise of Professional Society*, London: Routledge.

Perkin, H. (1996) *The Third Revolution: Professional Elites in the Modern World*, London: Routledge.

Walker, S.P. (1996) 'The criminal upperworld and the emergence of a disciplinary code in the early chartered accountancy profession', paper presented to the Department of Accounting and Financial Management, University of Essex, May 1996.

2

BEYOND THE ECONOMICS OF PROFESSIONALISM

Michael Dietrich and Jennifer Roberts

INTRODUCTION

This chapter concerns itself with two broad issues. The first of these is to investigate whether there is a uniquely economic approach to professionalism, and the second combines sociological and economic analyses to establish a more complete understanding of professional organisation. In relation to the first of these issues, we find that there does appear to be an economic rationale for professional organisation which, if disrupted, will result in significant welfare losses to both consumers and producers of services. Conventional economic analyses of professional organisation place stress on principal-agent and quality maintenance problems. It is argued below that such arguments do not provide a justification for professionalism *per se*, rather than, for instance, state regulation and individual contracts. Therefore, in this chapter the justification for professionalism is constructed in terms of informational complexity in combination with traditional economic preoccupations.

To introduce the second set of issues, it is argued that an inevitable trade-off exists between efficiency gains and power: more effective (professional) organisation embeds the power of professionals which if challenged leads to deteriorating efficiency advantages. This possibility leads us to the conclusion that an economic approach is inevitably incomplete. In particular the trade-off between professional efficiency and power can be managed by understanding the sociological bases of power. Hence our discussion is combined with the sociological literature in this area. Broadly speaking the sociological context provides an explanation of the way in which power is institutionalised, whereas the economic focus is necessary to maintain a role for individual agency.

The link between structure and agency is constructed on the basis of a professional ethic that institutionalises power. A professional ethic channels behaviour by requiring social recognition to be effective and in addition individual agency reinforces power relationships. This emphasis on structure and agency provides each profession with a unique historical

14

dynamic. To generalise these arguments we suggest a professional life-cycle based on structure-agency interaction.

ECONOMIC APPROACHES TO PROFESSIONALISM

Our initial approach is that common in economics: we undertake an intellectual exercise by starting with free markets and analysing the problems that are likely in situations characteristic of professional activity. This is purely an analytical process; we are not suggesting that professional organisation developed this way historically.

The search for a definition of professions and professionalism has not traditionally been a subject for economic analysis, rather economists have focused their concern on the characteristics of the markets for professional services. In particular they have searched for a justification for the departure from free market provision of services that professions have established. For economists there are two relevant features of professional markets. First, the issue of 'self-regulation' or the existence of a professional body that controls entry and enforces standards that are meant to promote quality. Second, the fact that professional activities have significant externalities. In general terms externalities exist when there are direct effects of production/consumption activities that are not accounted for in an exchange of goods or services. Classic examples are, of course, pollution (an external bad) and education-training (an external good). In terms of professional activity an obvious example is that of medical care; the treatment of a contagious disease confers general benefits over and above those enjoyed by the direct patient. In addition we can also think of the maintenance of justice, when legal professionals represent individual clients, and the effectiveness of contract law depending on the activities of accountants.

To understand these issues in an economic sense it is necessary to define free markets, and this can be approached in two stages. The market aspect can be defined as 'an exchange of property rights'. This is a definition that is used in much economic theory although it is often only made explicit by the 'property rights' school of thought.[1] Using this meaning it is clear that the purchase and sale of cars is a market transaction but the exchange of medical services in the public sector is not because of the absence of property rights. This difference is important because only with an exchange of property rights will individually based incentives for efficiency exist for both buyers and sellers. Without the constraints of ownership, principal-agent incentive problems can arise (as discussed later in this chapter). An implication here is that either we must introduce 'proper' markets (rather than what might be called pseudo alternatives) or we must have systems that generate social (rather than individual) efficiency. The 'free' part of 'free market' can be described in terms of two factors: (1) full information, i.e. prices conveying all information that is needed by buyers and sellers to assess the desirability of a purchase/sale; and (2) free entry and exit to eliminate monopoly power. One implication here is that market exchange is anonymous, therefore it follows that we do not need to know the individual characteristics of an economic agent, i.e. professional reputation is unimportant.

Given these definitions and introductory points we can begin to understand the economic rationale for professional organisation. The first point to realise is that this form of organisation is not unique, in a theoretical sense, but rather is a specific example of a more general set of issues that present problems for free-market economics. These issues revolve around two factors: policing of agreements and decision-making complexity. In general, free-market economics assumes (often implicitly) that policing issues are resolved by actual or potential recourse to legal sanction. While this may be the case in some circumstances it is not a general solution to the real problem of policing agreements. As important, in a conceptual sense, are non-legal methods of policing (Williamson, 1985), perhaps most importantly recourse to third-party (expert) conciliation and bilateral solutions that may involve authority or mutual negotiation. Non-legal methods of policing involve long-run, continuing economic relationships in which commitment and perhaps trust play an important role. This characterisation is in stark contrast to anonymous and essentially short-run free-market organisation supported by legal sanction. It is no accident, nor the result of a benevolent human nature, that non-legal policing occurs. Legal sanction will in general rupture an economic relationship and hence destroy any relationship-specific investments (human and fixed), this implies that there are non-trivial (opportunity) costs involved over and above the direct costs of legal activity. Hence in some cases it is more efficient to avoid recourse to court-ordered policing.

The problems just discussed take on an increasing significance when issues of decision-making complexity are introduced. Apart from the most trivial of examples, human beings are incapable of pre-thinking all issues involved with a decision because of the complexities involved – this is what Simon (1957, 1972) calls 'bounded rationality'. The implication here is that contracts and agreements are incomplete for most economic activity with problems resolved by learning and adaptation rather than full ex-ante specification (Dietrich, 1996). Effective learning and adaptation are profound reasons for continuing, rather than transient, relationships and hence the avoidance of legal activity.[2]

We will see that professionalism has no economic basis if decision-making complexity does not exist and if all policing is based on individual legal sanction. To discuss these issues in more detail we can make more direct reference to the economic literature on professional activity. Begun (1986) has identified two economic approaches to professionalism: the free-market approach and the market failure approach. The first of these suggests that professionalism arises due to the concentrated nature of producer interests relative to the diffuse nature of consumers (see, for example, Friedman, 1962; Stigler, 1971; Posner, 1974). Since the economic benefits of professionalism accrue only to the members of the profession, they have an incentive to mobilise and bear the costs of lobbying for their own economic interests. Without wishing to suggest that differential power is not an inevitable aspect of professional organisation (as discussed in this and other chapters) the free-market approach is partial in that there is no analysis of the implications of adopting free-market solutions for activities currently characterised by professional organisation.

The strength of the market failure approach to professionalism is that it stresses the (welfare) costs of free-market solutions, as discussed shortly, and hence identifies a positive set of reasons for professional organisation. However, from the perspective of the present chapter a major shortcoming of this latter approach is that it fails to acknowledge the power implications of professionalisation. Hence it is stressed here that both power and market failure are important. This combination presents problems for a narrowly defined economic approach because confronting power issues involves welfare costs, but minimising welfare costs (potentially) exacerbates professional power. To disentangle this conundrum it is necessary, in later sections of the chapter, to look outside economics.

The main justification for professionalism, from a market failure perspective, is that a seller/provider of a good or service has more (relevant) information than a buyer/user. This information asymmetry may disrupt the principle of *caveat emptor* (buyer beware). Hence 'delegation and trust are the social institutions designed to obviate the problem of informational inequality' (Arrow, 1963: 966). Information problems are a central aspect of the analysis of professionalism suggested below, but we would agree with Matthews (1991) that information asymmetries on their own are not a justification for professionalism. As discussed shortly, the economic principal-agent literature suggests that appropriately structured individual contracts (i.e. a free-market solution) can be used to overcome information disadvantages. Hence other factors must exist, in combination with information problems, to justify professionalism.

Leffler (1978) and Matthews (1991) introduce the existence of externalities (an important characteristic of professional activities) to provide this missing link. However, in principle externalities can be accommodated by individual negotiation with full property rights (Coase, 1960) or government tax/subsidy policies or regulation. There is no necessary link between, on the one hand, information problems and externalities and, on the other hand, professionalism. To derive such a link requires a more detailed examination of information problems, which is undertaken below. Leffler (1978) also suggests that consumers underestimate the risks of low quality service and hence derives a paternal argument for professionalism. We would claim two problems here: first, there is an uneasy association between a paternal argument for professionalism and the economic individualism of information problems. In other words paternalism is a partial move away from methodological individualism. A more complete move might ask *why* the low quality assessments exist, one answer might link them with a professional monopoly over information. Hence from a systemic perspective, low quality assessments and information problems can be seen as part of a wider perspective but not a justification for professionalism in themselves.

Other market failure arguments are suggested by Leland (1979) and Shapiro (1983). Here quality and professionalism are linked; rather than consumers simply underestimating the risks of low quality service, they are more generally thought to be sensitive to quality variations, and to value quality highly. In addition, quality and training are closely related, and there is a lower marginal cost of producing quality with well trained suppliers of a service. The problem with explanations such as these is that they describe professionalism rather than identifying its rationale. For example, it might be possible to guarantee quality with legally imposed minimum standards rather than autonomous professionals. The reasons for the latter existing, rather than the former, is an important matter we now discuss.

PRINCIPAL–AGENT PROBLEMS AND THE NATURE OF INFORMATION

This brief survey of the literature suggests that economists can identify the economic characteristics of professional organisation but find it difficult to identify the rationale for professionalism, rather than other forms of organisation. To derive this specific rationale we will investigate the nature of information problems in more detail. The economics of principal–agent relationships[3] provides a general framework in which a principal (in our case the consumer of services) has problems motivating an agent (the supplier of services) because of an information asymmetry to the agent's advantage. The central issue, as suggested above, is that in some circumstances information problems may be solved using free markets. We will aim to identify when this will not be possible.

Two types of principal–agent problems exist, hidden information and hidden action, and these have different characteristic solutions. Hidden information, also called adverse selection (after Akerlof, 1970), involves consumers/users not being able to identify the characteristics of a good/service before purchase/use but this information becomes evident during/after use. This hidden information problem has a parallel from a producer's perspective. If we have a number of competing firms (for example, legal companies not constrained by professional regulation), and consumers cannot effectively distinguish between these firms in terms of quality, then quality degradation by one firm (to increase short-run profits) will negatively impact on the activities of competitors even if they are maintaining high quality standards.

From a corporate perspective this quality degradation problem can be resolved by vertical integration (Williamson, 1981); for example, in the professional context, a company having its own internal law department to provide legal services. From this perspective there is no necessary link with professionalisation. But as a general solution, particularly for consumer services, integration is not appropriate. In certain circumstances individually based arms-length contracting can be used to motivate any principal. This involves paying high quality agents a premium over that payable to degraders such that the services delivered by reputable producers are less than they potentially could produce (hence embodying a monopoly payoff) but are more than those that low quality suppliers are willing to generate.

This solution nests into professional regulation and policing of suppliers with monopoly returns. Hence quality degradation, limited by professional organisation with internal accountability and punishment, can, if successful, generate an effective guarantee to consumers. The related supplier power provides a payoff to professionals for agreeing to institutionalised accountability and control. While this reasoning identifies a possible rationale for professionalisation, in the context of hidden information, it fails to identify a specific rationale. In particular two gaps are evident in the reasoning: what factors inhibit market based control of quality problems; and how might the institutionalisation processes take place. An economic perspective on these gaps will be provided shortly. A more complete analysis will be suggested in later sections.

Information problems based on hidden action (originally analysed by Arrow (1962) in the context of the insurance market and termed 'moral hazard') involve the principal not being able to observe the actions, or significance of the actions, taken by an agent, with obvious possibilities for abuse. The solution involves a contract that has both payments and penalties. The latter are invoked when an agent attempts to abuse the non-observability of actions and are of sufficient size to inhibit any shirking behaviour.[4] This formulation has an intuitive appeal in terms of describing a rationale for professional control. But we are faced with the same gaps in the reasoning as suggested in the previous paragraph: what inhibits markets and how might institutionalisation occur.

To render market based solutions to principal–agent problems possible a number of rather counter-intuitive assumptions are necessary. Principals must not be able to observe the actions (or implications of the actions) of an agent (or in the context of hidden information, the characteristics of an agent) but the following are assumed to be observable and under-standable: the output produced, the preferences/aspirations of the agent, and the transformation/production process undertaken. Without knowledge of the latter factors it is impossible to develop an effective agent-specific contract. It might seem appropriate to suggest that in some circumstances such knowledge might be generally available or can be generated during (costly) negotiation processes. But, even ignoring the problems involved with strategic revelation of information during negotiation, there is an additional issue that is particularly relevant in terms of our discussion.

We are considering the economic basis of professional services. The identifying characteristic of services is that production and consumption processes coincide, which implies that the outputs produced and the transformation processes cannot be separated. With hidden action an inability to understand the significance of actions taken feeds forward into an ignorance of the transformation process which in turn implies an ignorance of the output produced. With hidden information an inability to identify the characteristics of an agent feeds backwards into ignorance of transformation processes. An aspect of this inevitable ignorance problem is frequently highlighted, in debates over the relevance of recent changes to public sector management in the UK, in terms of an inability to develop appropriate performance indicators for financial rather than professional control because of an inability to measure output. But this inability is an aspect of a much wider ignorance about the characteristics of actions, transformation processes and outputs. Even if output could be effectively measured (for example, by producing league tables to demonstrate school performance) the significance of any results would be difficult to assess because of 'upstream' ignorance.

To link this principal–agent problem to professional organisation involves delving into the nature of ignorance in more detail. Ignorance is not simply a *lack* of information, but also an inability to use the information that is available. This inability depends on the difficulty, or ease, of information transfer. Following Winter (1987) we can suggest that the difficulties or costs of transferring information will be a function of three major factors:[5] the tacitness of information, the observability of information, and the extent to which an element of information is independent or part of a system.

The importance of tacitness was first suggested by Polanyi (1962a, b, 1967). Two types of information can be (rather schematically) distinguished: communicable and tacit. Communicable knowledge can be codified and effectively articulated by arms-length contact; for example, such information can be put on the Internet and any reader can understand its significance. Tacit knowledge cannot be fully expressed and is therefore uncodified – in the words of Polanyi (1962b) 'there are things that we know but cannot tell' (p. 601). A useful example is the ability to play a musical instrument. More generally any activity that involves skill or expertise development, or learning by doing, is based on tacit knowledge. Many professionals acquire a large degree of diagnostic knowledge that cannot be learnt from books. An important characteristic is that this type of tacit knowledge can only be understood in the context of particular actions, and may be shared to a significant degree by individuals who have a common (professional) experience. The fact that most individual consumers will use a particular professional service relatively infrequently, will contribute to this problem, since it implies not only insufficient experience to understand actions, but also that any accumulated experience will depreciate between uses.[6]

The observability of information involves the extent to which underlying information must be disclosed in order for it to be used. To some extent this might be the result of secrecy and monopoly control but, even ignoring these issues, a common characteristic of professional activities is that this observability is not present. We allow professional autonomy which implies non-observability of processes. Finally, there is the extent to which an element of information is independent or part of a system. This has obvious relevance to professional services (for example, medicine) or more generally when expert advice is sought.

We can link these three factors that determine the transferability (or otherwise) of information to our earlier discussion of decision-making complexity. We can define complexity (or simplicity) as the amount of information that is necessary to make effective decisions. Tacitness and the systemic nature of any information will directly increase the complexity involved. Non-observability implies that information acquisition involves additional (search and acquisition) activities, with their own decision-making requirements, and hence indirectly increases the complexity of decision making.

The link between principal–agent problems and professionalism can now be seen to involve the (non) transferability of information. If information is transferable (or decision making not complex), ignorance can be effectively overcome by information search and acquisition processes. In such circumstances league tables and the like are relevant, with the only factor inhibiting communication being secrecy. It follows that, with sufficient information in the public arena, principal–agent problems can be solved on the basis of individual contracts and financial incentives. But with barriers to information transfer, significant costs must be incurred for information to be understandable and usable. A useful example might be that the only way that an individual can understand the significance of medical information (outputs and transformation processes) is with a medical training: in such circumstances it would be true to say that a little knowledge *is* a bad thing. With non-transferable information individual

21

contracts cannot be used to overcome principal–agent problems because of the fundamental ignorance of principals. What is required is the guarantee offered by professionalism so that ignorant principals can trust the agents to behave in appropriate ways.

A recurrent theme in this discussion of professionalism is that its existence embodies monopoly power. This is also the case with principal–agent issues. To independently control a professionally organised activity requires the information used by professionals. The acquisition of such information involves sunk costs (the expenditures generate no tangible asset which can be sold to recoup outlays) because of learning, system understanding and the costs of acquiring (directly) non-observable information. As with all sunk costs they imply non-contestable activities with the corresponding monopoly power (Baumol, 1982). This result is to some extent a pessimistic one: as mentioned earlier, the more effectively a principal–agent problem is resolved by effective professional regulation the more entrenched will be professional activity, and therefore monopoly power. An obvious conclusion is therefore that individually based *economic* accountability is not relevant because its development implies worsening principal-agent problems. Even the provision of alternative information sources is not relevant because the information involved will also be non-transferable with its problems of understanding. In this light the importance of trust and continuing relationships is obvious. But even trust does not remove the differential power relationship, it simply makes it manageable.

SOCIOLOGICAL APPROACHES TO PROFESSIONALISM

An economic rationale for professional organisation has been established but the economic approach is incomplete because it says nothing about possible institutionalisation processes that are necessary for professionals to emerge. Relatedly, although it enables us to establish the inevitable trade-off between efficiency gains and power in the professional context, it does not enable any meaningful analysis of the power relationships embodied in professional activity, beyond a limited economistic understanding of monopoly power in exchange. In order to do this we must complement our economic analysis with sociological approaches to professionalism, which can be classified broadly as either taxonomic or power approaches.

The taxonomic approach is a body of literature which asserts that professions are a special category of occupations which possess unique attributes that distinguish them from other non-professional occupations (Carr-Saunders, 1928; Goode, 1960). Johnson (1972) further distinguishes between two taxonomic strands suggesting that the trait approach centres on the formulation of lists of attributes which are not theoretically related, but which are seen to characterise professions, whereas in a less abstract way, the structural-functionalist approach focuses on those attributes that are seen to be functional to wider society. This distinction is not necessary for our purposes and it is sufficient to consider definitions such as that employed by Crompton (1987), the Monopolies and Mergers Commission (UK) (1970) and Millerson (1964), as emerging from the taxonomic approach. Here the particular characteristics seen as important include the possession of specialised skills, the necessity of intellectual and practical training and the perceived collective responsibility for maintaining the integrity of the profession as a whole organised via a professional body.

One of the main criticisms of this taxonomic view is that it merely provides a description of professions, not a basis for analysis. Specifically it takes no account of the unequal distribution of power between professionals and consumers of professional services. Functionalists view the relationship between the professions and society simply as an exchange. The professions provide specialised knowledge and skills, and in return they are rewarded with autonomy, high income and status. Access to these privileges promotes the entry of highly qualified and well-motivated individuals which maintains quality standards. This obscures the historical conditions under which occupational groups become professions – the unique professionalisation projects of different occupations.

In direct contrast, the power approach claims that the distinguishing feature of the professions is purely their ability to gain societal recognition as professions. This approach emerged from the Chicago school of symbolic interactionists (Atkinson, 1983; Freidson, 1983) who argue that professions are essentially the same as other occupations. There is no precise and unique definition of professions; it is merely a title claimed by certain occupations at certain points in time. The important factor here is the recognition that professional rewards are sufficient for occupations to seek them; that is, to strive for professional status. The relevant question, therefore, is not to determine what a profession is in the absolute sense, but rather to consider how society determines who and what is professional? (MacDonald and Ritzer, 1988)

Within the power approach most work can be classified as either Marxist or neo-Weberian. The Marxist analysis of professions centres on the social relations of production and emerged, in part, from the need to locate the middle classes in the class system. There is a broad spectrum of opinion concerning the position of professionals; at one extreme professions are seen as a means of articulating the state and fulfilling the global functions of capitalism (Johnson, 1977; Poulantzas, 1975), while at the other they are seen as subject to proletarianisation and de-skilling, gradually losing status and power (Braverman, 1974). In addition, Wright (1985) has argued that professions are a 'contradictory location within class relations' sharing characteristics with the exploited and the exploiters. Professional groups will attempt to use their power as exploiters to gain entry to the dominant exploiting class, and in turn this will strengthen their professional position.

The neo-Weberian literature focuses on market conditions, viewing society as an arena where competing groups struggle with each other, and the state, to gain power and status. Conflict is a catalyst for change and the segmented nature of occupations that strive for professional status is crucial to this process. Segmentation creates a diversity of needs and wants, which are central to forming an occupation's experience of professionalisation. The struggle for control is facilitated through social closure, which is employed by professional groups to defend their privileged position (Parkin, 1979; Freidson, 1970). Professionals struggle to achieve market control by restricting entry to a limited group of eligibles (Larson, 1977). Eligibility is primarily based on credentialism and is often backed by legislation such as registration under statute.

In terms of our own analysis the most important contribution of both the Marxist and neo-Weberian work on professionalism is its explicitly dynamic approach. The central role of conflict and struggle, and the need to achieve and consolidate professional status, necessitates historical analysis of professional organisation in stark contrast to the static, ahistorical approach that characterises the economic literature. Central to this historical analysis is a recognition of the power sources utilised by occupations in their struggle to achieve and maintain professional status, and the way this power is institutionalised within the emerging profession.

BEYOND THE ECONOMICS OF PROFESSIONS

One initial similarity between the economic and sociological approaches is their incompleteness. The economic analysis can establish a rationale for professional organisation based on informational complexity and traditional principal-agent problems. However, it then fails to provide any analytical basis for understanding the power that inevitably emerges from professional organisation, particularly the way this power is institutionalised, even though it can demonstrate that disrupting this power will cause efficiency losses. Early taxonomic sociological literature recognised that professions may have a functional rationale, but it fell short of defining precisely what this rationale might be. In addition the Marxist and neo-Weberian sociological literature recognises the central role of struggle and hence historical analysis of professional organisation, but again this fails to establish a rationale for the emergence of professional organisation.

By drawing on elements from both the economic and sociological perspectives we can provide a more complete analysis of professions and professionalisation. An existing attempt to link economic and sociological approaches is provided by Begun (1986) who recognises a potentially useful complementarity likening the taxonomic sociological approach to the market failure approach in economics, and the power approach to the economic free-market approach. However, he does not sufficiently develop the linkages between these two different literatures, and we argue that a more explicit coverage of their different analytical approaches is necessary in order to facilitate this.

Links between the sociological structural-functionalist approach and the market failure approach of economics emerge from the fact that the functional rationale for professions is as a response to the types of market failure and informational complexity identified above. On its own the sociological structural-functionalist analysis of professions is somewhat lacking, and the taxonomic definitions collapse into mere descriptions of existing professions. However, by drawing on the economic analysis developed above, we can identify a unique functional rationale for professions based on decision-making complexity which cannot be solved via individual contracts due to the non-transferability of information.

In another attempt to link the literatures, Begun (1986) draws similarities between the free-market economic view of professions and the power perspective in sociology. This link is particularly tenuous and the concept of power is particularly problematic in this respect, because power is defined and understood very differently from within the two disciplines. The role of competition is central to these arguments since it can provide a basis for power from within both economic and sociological perspectives. In neo-classical economics competition is viewed as a structure, and is defined in relation to markets. Hence power from an economic standpoint really refers to power in exchange, and the economic free-market approach to professions is based on the concept of the monopoly power of professionals, which arises from their control of entry to the market. The definition of power as a process is more consistent with sociological approaches. Hence the power perspective in sociology is concerned with a profession's ability to access and maintain power in order to lay claim to professional status. We would argue that, to provide a rationale for professions, power must be understood in both structural and processual senses.

It follows that power plays a pivotal role in understanding the role and nature of professional activity. The structural bases of economic power are only possible to maintain, in a social context, if divergent relations of dominance are reproduced in social practices. Without the latter processual supports to professional power, we can learn from Austrian economics that inequalities in exchange would have no long-run viability. This dual, intersecting role of structure and process is illustrated particularly well in the context of professional ethics. The issue of ethics has been problematic for both economists and sociologists. The existing literature is insufficient in that the rationale for professional ethics appears to reduce to a simple psychological explanation. Rather we believe that ethics have a fundamental role in linking individual decision-making processes to the social context in which they operate, and in order to explain this we must look at the distinct concerns of economics and sociology.

The philosophical basis of free-market economics (whether in neo-classical or Austrian versions) is methodological individualism. The individual is seen as the fundamental unit of economic analysis, and through the activity of these individual units, the functioning of the economy is explained. This approach assigns logical priority to micro over macro, and statements about aggregate phenomena must be grounded in and derived from an analysis of individual behaviour. In contrast socio-logical analysis is concerned with the social context of individual behav-iour. Furthermore, individual behaviour is only meaningful within the context of society. Society is viewed as more than simply a group of individuals, and societal structures emerge which are not based purely on an aggregation of individual decision-making processes.

The individualistic basis of economic analysis is limited as a framework for consideration of professional ethics. To the extent that these exist and govern professional behaviour they must, by definition, have a social context. The existing economic literature has questioned whether or not a professional ethic exists, in that professionals have distinct objective functions from people involved in business (Matthews, 1991; Foley et al., 1981). This economic approach to professional ethics is unsatisfactory since it has no wider social context; the ethic is seen as a psychological individual phenomenon, it is not viewed as having meaning that is created within the social context. In professional markets, ethics should be seen as socially constructed individual decisions, and hence cannot be analysed from a purely economic standpoint. It follows that professional ethics are the filter through which economic and social power mutually reinforce each other. Without social status, as recognised in a professional ethic, the potential offered by economic power cannot be realised. Without an economic basis social recognition, and the power this engenders, has no context.

Of course, the link between the individual and the social created by professional ethics is only, in theory, 'pure' with no 'control loss'. Rather we prefer to view ethics on a continuum ranging from purely indi-vidualistic to purely socially constructed, and this can be applied to all occupations. Decision making in professions is placed closer to the socially constructed end of the spectrum whereas decision making in non-professional business is closer to the purely individualistic end. In short, there is no unique professional ethic; it is simply that professionals are involved in areas where the significant externalities involved in trans-actions warrant broader social constraints on behaviour. The acceptance of these constraints is necessary in order to gain social recognition as a profession.

To avoid confusion it may be as well to point out that it is not being suggested that as one moves closer to individual economic relationships there is an automatic increase in the equality of social relationships. As Marx (1867) recognised, claims of equality in economic exchange ignore the substantively greater inequalities in control over production (or strategic decisions in modern language). Potential economic power can be realised in ways other than a reliance on a professional ethic. For example, position in an organisational hierarchy; the responsibilities of trade unions; the ability to undertake effective negotiation, policing and lobbying of economic and political actors; expectations of behaviour based on gender and racial identity are all important in terms of linking economic and social dominance. In general terms, therefore, economic power always requires a social structure, with characteristic socially defined behaviour, to be effective. This chapter is merely concerned with a small sub-set of the totality of behaviours, i.e. professionalism. But, as discussed shortly, to understand the institutionalisation of professional activity requires a recognition of the ways in which professional bases of power intersect with other aspects of socially defined behaviour.

Having set out the important idea of an intersecting economic and social context, we should guard against an overly static framework with no real human agency. The environment within which professions operate is not static. The professionals themselves, through their individual behaviour, play a role in forming the social context. We can think of ethics as providing the link between the individual professional and the professions as institutions that have a role and position in wider society. The individual decision-making processes undertaken by professionals are constrained by the fact that the professions are a societally recognised institution; this is ethically constrained professional behaviour. However, individual decision-making also has feedback effects in continually reshaping professional institutions. In addition individual professionals and professional institutions are also operating within a wider environment in which the state, class and gender relations and other societal institutions such as the family and trade unions also play a role in modifying and constraining behaviour.

This leads inevitably to historically specific, dynamic analyses of professional organisation as the only way to explain why some occupations have professional status and others do not. Not only is this type of analysis necessary to understand the emergence of professions, but it is also necessary to understand why professional status is not a static concept. Existing professions can lose status, new professions can emerge and the nature of professionalism itself can change. These arguments are developed in relation to specific professions throughout the chapters of this book, and here we attempt to generalise them in terms of a life-cycle model of the professions.

The emergence of professions requires an economic rationale but once a profession has emerged, the ability to maintain and develop professional status involves social recognition. Nursing for example, while it seems to possess the necessary attributes of an economic profession, has been unable to achieve the shift to core professional status. There are many factors underlying the inability of nursing to gain social recognition as a profession despite its existing economic rationale, and the sex composition of the occupation is a central issue (Witz, 1992). In similar fashion, core professional status can be undermined by institutional, organisational and technical changes. The accounting activity of auditing is currently experiencing this shift, based on technical changes that have led to a routinisation of the audit process and organisational changes that have removed the information asymmetry traditionally present in a professional-client relationship. Hence auditing has lost the economic rationale for professional status, but nevertheless it is still an accounting task and at present still clings to a sociological rationale. There is evidence, though, that this is gradually changing and auditing is losing status within the accounting profession; a survey in the UK professional publication *Accountancy* in 1988 revealed that few high quality accountants see auditing as an inviting and rewarding career, compared with the alternatives such as management consultancy, fund management and other financial services. Clear evidence for the low status of auditing within the accounting profession is also provided by the qualitative research of Hanlon in chapter 8 of this volume.

To avoid purely mechanistic reasoning, it is also necessary to recognise that professionals are agents of change, and have a degree of control over institutional and organisational development. Again this is illustrated by the changing position of auditing, since it has been argued that the accounting profession as a whole is responsible for the reduction in auditors' status (Roberts and Coutts, 1992). The differentiation of auditing from other accountancy services has been partly a response to the feminisation of this area and the potential threat to professional status that this brings.

CONCLUSION

This chapter has argued that to construct a coherent economics of professional organisation requires a movement beyond traditional considerations of principal-agent and quality issues. The core economic aspect of professional activity is the non-transferability of information used in the client-agent relationship. The resulting introduction of decision-making complexity resolves one issue but introduces a problem in that the acquisition of information in complex conditions involves sunk costs of decision making; as with all sunk costs, relationships become non-perfectly contestable, with issues of power being endemic. These theoretical issues have been conceptualised in terms of a trade-off between efficiency and power: the resolution of efficiency problems reinforces power which if challenged damages efficiency characteristics.

The investigation of this efficiency-power trade moved this chapter into a consideration of sociological approaches to professional activity. The logic here was that if the potential offered by economic power is to be realised the dominance involved must be sociologically recognised. Lack of such recognition, or the absence of an economic rationale, introduced important complexities into the functioning and significance of professional activity. The link between individual activity and the social context was created in terms of a functioning professional ethic. A well established ethic is only possible with an economic and sociological basis to professional activity and allows the monopoly position to function effectively.

The interaction between the individual and the social context was conceptualised in terms of a professional life-cycle. Given an economic rationale the creation of a professional ethic involves agents in the sociological construction of their profession. This creation inevitably introduces issues of the bases upon which professional power can be constructed. In a modern context we can see the dynamics involved here with certain 'emerging' professions: for instance management consultancy, marketing, personnel management and the like. The struggles involved here illustrate two key features of the arguments developed. First, the development of professional power is frequently undertaken on the basis of alliance creation with existing professions. So, for example, management consultancy seems to 'attach itself' to accounting and legal activity to gain the social credibility involved. Second, the bases of power reflect wider power differentials. It is perhaps more difficult for personnel managers to gain professional status because of an increasing preponderance of women in this activity. These comments are, of course, merely suggestive of how the approach developed in this paper might be used to analyse the dynamics of professional activity. More complete investigation obviously involves detailed case-study and historical investigation.

Finally in this conclusion we might turn to a brief consideration of the policy implications of the arguments developed. At a first level it might seem appropriate to distinguish between private and public sector activities. In the private sector property rights are well defined and the resulting incentives imply that professionalism and the resulting monopoly power will result in financial gain and incomplete access to the services to those with insufficient resources. In the public sector access will not depend on ability to pay but professionalism still implies monopoly power – with no exchange of property rights when services are delivered monopoly power

29

is likely to involve a wider set of issues than simply financial gain: independence and autonomy of decision making might be important. In both cases a challenge to professional power is likely to have adverse consequences. In the private sector these might include more obvious commercial opportunism and costs of legal policing. In the public sector introducing a private sector managerial logic to challenge professionalism without real market processes will simply lead to a transfer of power from one set of actors to another.

This formulation allows us to suggest the following conclusions. If private sector professionalism is based on non-transferable information and social recognition, the major object of policy should not be oriented towards the professionalism itself but rather the incomplete economic and social access involved. Public funding and voluntary activity might be appropriate here in terms of making, for example, legal services more accountable to public demand. In the public sector the important issue would seem to be how to render professionals more accountable. We have argued that an economic or financial logic is not appropriate here. The economic or decision-making power of professionals must be recognised in terms of a solution to quality and principal-agent issues. But this does not imply that public sector professionals should single-handedly control the strategic agenda, i.e. the framework within which services are produced. Any single locus of strategic authority in a non-market setting will generate non-accountability. It is empty to debate which decision-making authority is in some sense best because each will embody its own particular objectives which render universal comparison impossible. The only solution is to make the strategic authority itself more accountable which should be recognised as a socio-political as much as an economic issue.

NOTES

1 The 'property rights' school of thought in economics is based on the principle that overall economic efficiency depends on a complete specification of property rights (for all goods and services including externalities) and individual incentives based on legal sanction. Representative statements in this tradition are Coase (1960), Demsetz (1967) and Alchian and Demsetz (1972). While we adopt, in the text, a property rights definition of markets we do not accept the free-market conclusions, for reasons developed below.

2 A secondary-point is that complexity, as discussed in the text, implies the ignorance of economic agents rather than just risky decisions that are accommodated by forms of insurance. With risk, the only uncertainty is how the future will evolve (the 'state of the world' as economists call it) but in each possible state of the world complete cost-benefit calculation is undertaken and hence is fully understood.

3 Our coverage is intuitive, and more technical discussions of principal-agent theory (upon which the claims in the text are based) can be found in many

intermediate-advanced microeconomic texts (for example, Gravelle and Rees, 1992; Kreps, 1990).

4 A technical point is that a contractually based solution to hidden action may not be possible with high degrees of agent risk aversion. This is because of the (perceived) demotivating effects of adverse environmental factors causing a penalty to be invoked (rather than the shirking of the agent). It is arguably inappropriate, however, to base a universal theory of professionalism on the slender thread of individual risk aversion.

5 The presentation in the text departs from Winter (1987) in two respects. First, he makes reference to the transferability of knowledge. The differences between knowledge and information involve epistemological and ontological matters beyond the scope of this paper. The term information is used in the text because it is standard in economics. Second, Winter highlights complexity as a separate, independent factor (making four major factors) that determine knowledge/information transferability. In the text we suggest that complexity is the result of the other (three) factors.

6 This idea of depreciating experience is due to Nelson and Winter (1982).

REFERENCES

Akerlof, G.A. (1970) 'The market for 'lemons': Quality, uncertainty and the market mechanism', *Quarterly Journal of Economics*, 84, 488–500.

Alchian, A.A. and Demsetz, H. (1972) 'Production, information costs, and economic organization', *American Economic Review*, 62, 777–95.

Arrow, K.J. (1962) 'Economic welfare and the allocation of resources for invention', in *The Rate and Direction of Inventive Activity: Economic and Social Factors*, National Bureau of Economic Research, Princeton University Press: 609–25. Reprinted in D.M. Lamberton (ed.) (1971), *Economics of Information and Knowledge*, Harmondsworth: Penguin.

Arrow, K.J. (1963) 'Uncertainty and the welfare economics of medical care', *American Economic Review*, 53, 941–73.

Atkinson, P. (1983) 'The reproduction of the professional community', in R. Dingwall and P. Lewis (eds) *The Sociology of Professions*, London: Macmillan.

Baumol, W.J. (1982) 'Contestable markets: an uprising in the theory of industrial structure', *American Economic Review*, 72, 1–15.

Begun, J.W. (1986) 'Economic and sociological approaches to professionalism', *Work and Occupations*, 13, 113–29.

Braverman, H. (1974) *Labour and Monopoly Capital: The Degradation of Work in the Twentieth Century*, New York: Monthly Review Press.

Carr-Saunders, A.M. (1928) 'Professionalisation in historical perspective', in H.M. Vollmer and D. Mills (eds) *Professionalisation*, Englewood Cliffs: Prentice-Hall.

Coase, R.H. (1960) 'The problem of social cost', *Journal of Law and Economics*, 3, 1–44.

Crompton, R. (1987) 'Gender and accountancy: A response to Tinker and Neimark', *Accounting, Organizations and Society*, 103–10.

Demsetz, H. (1967) 'Towards a theory of property rights', *American Economic Review (proceedings)*, 57, 347–59.

Dietrich, M. (1996) 'Opportunism, learning and organisational evolution', in J. Groenewegen (ed.) *Transaction Cost Economics and Beyond*, Kluwer Publishers, forthcoming.

Foley, P., Shaked, A. and Sutton, J. (1981) *The Economics of the Professions: An Introduction to the Literature*, London: LSE.

Friedman, M. (1962) 'Occupational licensure', in M. Friedman (ed.) *Capitalism and Freedom*, Chicago: University of Chicago Press.

Freidson, E. (1970) *Profession of Medicine*, New York: Dodd Mead.

Freidson, E. (1983) 'The theory of the professions: the state of the art', in R. Dingwall and P. Lewis (eds) *The Sociology of the Professions: Lawyers, Doctors and Others*, New York: St Martins.

Goode, W.J. (1960) 'Encroachment, charlatanism and the emerging professions: psychology, medicine and sociology', *American Sociological Review*, 25: 902–14.

Gravelle, H. and Rees, R. (1992) *Microeconomics*, second edition, Harlow: Longman.

Hirschman, A.O. (1970) *Exit, Voice and Loyalty: Responses to Decline in Firms, Organizations and States*, Cambridge: Harvard University Press.

Johnson, T.J. (1972) *Professions and Power*, London: Macmillan.

Johnson, T.J. (1977) 'The professions in the class structure', in R. Scase (ed.) *Industrial Society: Class, Cleavage and Control*, Allen & Unwin.

Kreps, D.M. (1990), *A Course in Microeconomic Theory*, London: Harvester Wheatsheaf.

Larson, M.S. (1977) *The Rise of Professionalism*, Berkeley: University of California Press.

Leffler, K.B. (1978) 'Physician licensure: Competition and monopoly in American medicine', *Journal of Law and Economics*, 21, 165–86.

Leland, H.E. (1979) 'Quacks, lemons and licensing: A theory of minimum quality standards', *Journal of Political Economy*, 87, 1328–46.

MacDonald, K.M. and Ritzer, G. (1988) 'The sociology of professions: dead or alive', *Work and Occupations*, 15, 251–72.

Marx, K. (1867, reprinted 1976) *Capital*, 1, Harmondsworth: Penguin.

Matthews, R.C.O. (1991) 'The economics of professional ethics: Should the professions be more like business?', *The Economic Journal*, 101, 737–51.

Millerson, G.L. (1964) *The Qualifying Association*, London: Routledge & Kegan Paul.

Monopolies and Mergers Commission (UK) (1970) *A report on the general effect on the public interest of certain restrictive practices so far as they prevail in relation to the supply of professional services*, Cmnd 4463, London: HMSO.

Nelson, R.R. and Winter, S.G. (1982) *An Evolutionary Theory of Economic Change*, Boston: Harvard University Press.

Parkin, F. (1979) *Marxism and Class Theory: A Bourgeois Critique*, London: Tavistock.

Polanyi, M. (1962a) *Personal Knowledge: Towards a post-critical philosophy*, London: Harper & Row.

Polanyi, M. (1962b) 'Tacit knowledge: Its bearing on some problems of philosophy', *Reviews of Modern Physics*, 34.

Polanyi, M. (1967) *The Tacit Dimension*, London: Routledge & Kegan Paul.

Posner, R.A. (1974) 'Theories of economic regulation', *Bell Journal of Economics and Management Science*, 5, 335–58

Poulantzas, N. (1975) *Classes in Contemporary Capitalism*, London: New Left Books.

Roberts, J. and Coutts, J.A. (1992) 'Feminization and professionalization: A review of an emerging literature on the development of accounting in the United Kingdom', *Accounting, Organizations and Society*, 17, 379–95.

Shapiro, C. (1983) 'Occupational licensure as an input regulation', *Discussion Paper* 44, Woodrow Wilson School, Princeton University.

Simon, H.A. (1957) *Models of Man*, London: John Wiley & Sons Inc.

Simon, H.A. (1972) 'Theories of bounded rationality', in C. McGuire, and R. Radner (eds) *Decision and Organization*, Amsterdam: North-Holland.

Stigler, G.J. (1971) 'The theory of economic regulation', *Bell Journal of Economics and Management Science*, 2, 3–21.

Williamson, O.E. (1981) 'The modern corporation: Origins, evolution, attributes', *Journal of Economic Literature*, 19, 1537–68.

Williamson, O.E. (1985) *The Economic Institutions of Capitalism: Firms, Markets, Relational Contracting*, London: Macmillan.

Winter, S.G. (1987) 'Knowledge and competence as strategic assets', in D.J. Teece (ed.) *The Competitive Challenge: Strategies for Industrial Innovation and Renewal*, London: Harper & Row.

Witz, A. (1992) *Professions and Patriarchy*, London: Routledge.

Wright, E.O. (1985) *Classes*, New York: Verso.

3

'ACCOUNTING LOGIC' AND CONTROLLING PROFESSIONALS

The case of the public sector

Jane Broadbent and Richard Laughlin

INTRODUCTION

The aim of this chapter is to reflect on the role of accounting in attempts to develop controls over professionals. It seeks to provide a link between the ideas of economics and accounting and examine issues of control in a broad sense. A general theme is that many of the changes taking place, particularly in the UK public sector, are ones which have previously been under the control of professionals. The changes taking place are ones which we see as informed by 'accounting logic' and which claim their legitimacy through the application of market-type controls. One require-ment of the market approach is the possibility of defining what is to be subject to exchange and putting an exchange value on it. The theme of hierarchies, markets and clans (developed in the work of Williamson and Ouchi) will be used as a heuristic to frame the argument that the imposition of market-based controls is essentially ideological. It will be argued that accounting and 'accounting logic' is so centrally implicated because it provides the technology to operationalise the controls required to make a market possible. In order to do this the chapter will be structured in the following manner. First, the framework of markets, hierarchies and clans will be introduced. Second, the nature of accounting and 'accounting logic' will be explored. The question of how we characterise professions will be the third issue addressed and finally the implications of using market-type controls in a professional context will be examined. The chapter will use the areas of education and primary health care, where the authors have been engaged in extensive research, to provide illustrations of many of the issues discussed.

CHANGE IN THE PUBLIC SECTOR: AN OVERVIEW AND A FRAMEWORK FOR ANALYSIS

There has been a good deal of rhetoric about the ability of a more market-based approach to promote competition and efficiency in the public sector. The failure of the organisations which have been responsible for the provision of our public services has been bemoaned. In education the problem has been seen as a failure to provide the requisite workforce for the needs of the economy. This is seen to have led to the general failure of the Western economies *vis à vis* Japan. In the context of health the problem is the escalating cost. The desire has been to move areas of the public sector away from previous modes of control which were a mixture of bureaucratic lines of organisation in which some professional involvement was also central. The previous situation was one in which the emphasis in the administration of the services was on a hierarchical organisational structure and in which rules were developed to regularise the relationships of different post holders in the organisation. Accountability was through the application of checks on probity and stewardship of resource usage. Running alongside the hierarchical bureaucracy was a professional sphere of activity where the hierarchy was defined more by the professional relationships, for example in the NHS the relationships of doctors and nurses and of different types of doctors and nurses. Much of the control of professional activity was through the professional norms and values. The relationship with those who used the services was a complex one, but was not seen as a provider–customer relationship. Accountability was operated more through professional norms and it has been argued that this militated against the needs of individual users – pupils or patients, for example.

The rhetoric which has accompanied the changes has been one which has extolled the benefits of the market and competition and this, it has been argued, is to be the vehicle to promote efficiency and effectiveness. In an attempt to remedy the problems, there has been a delegation of responsibility to service units and central to this has been a delegation of *financial* responsibility. Behind this delegation is the implicit logic that individuals can make decisions about the way they organise the services, including how they can best use the resources available to provide best for local needs. Added to this is the desire to promote freedom for the users of services (the customers) to choose their supplier, thus providing some element of competition. The desire is that the resources should follow the 'consumer' and as customers can choose the provider then the providers who give what customers require (the 'best' providers) will thrive, whilst those who do not will wither. In the case of education, for example, the schools now control their own budgets and resources are largely allocated to schools on an age-weighted pupil basis. It is argued that successful schools will be the ones which will attract pupils and resources. Account-abilities still have to be provided in a market-based system and the notion of an accountability for outputs is important. For example, the publishing of league tables of examination results in schools provides accountability. Exam results are seen as the outputs of the education process and it is argued that they give information to allow choice about which school a child should attend. Where there is emphasis on the purchaser–provider split, the outputs – the services provided – which are 'sold', must also have a price attached to them and hence here there is a need to do this as well as define the output. This provides a further financial focus.

Whilst the actuality of the controls both before and after the reforms is not necessarily neatly categorised it is perhaps useful to reflect on them in a broad sense and the framework developed by Ouchi (1977, 1980) and the work of Williamson (1975) provides a good heuristic framework to allow this. It should be recognised that the framework is not intended to be wholly descriptive of the actuality, but to provide three 'ideal types' which characterise three different approaches to control.

Ouchi followed Williamson in differentiating markets and hierarchies. Williamson suggested, in turn using the work of Coase (1937), that the issue of costs was important in deciding whether transactions should be co-ordinated through the medium of the market or through an organ-isation. In a market situation the exchange takes place through the medium of a contract and if the cost of constantly contracting is greater than the cost of having the longer term contractual relationship found in organ-isational settings then logic suggests that an organisation should be developed. Williamson's work assumed that individuals in situations of complexity and uncertainty will have bounded rationality and display opportunistic behaviour and because of this contracts are costly. The extent of that cost will depend on the level of the uncertainty and complexity surrounding the transaction concerned as well as the pos-sibility of using the skills and assets which are involved in the transaction in other situations. If complexity is high and there is no alternative use for the skills and assets then the transaction costs are likely to be high and we might expect that an organisation (or hierarchy) would minimise the costs.

Ouchi (1980), in seeking to explore the problem of achieving co-operation between individuals with objectives which might not be the same (1980: 833), extended the categorisation, differentiating between markets, hierarchies and clans. Various elements decided the most appro-priate form of control. Two important ones are identified as the extent of the knowledge of the transformation process and the ability to measure outputs. Where organisations (hierarchies) or markets exist it is possible to control either through a knowledge of the transformation process (controlling behaviour) or by monitoring the outputs which are produced. We suggest that in a traditional bureaucracy there is likely to be a focus on the process, and that the rules and regulations which characterise a bureaucracy are likely to relate to the nature of the transformation process as well as to the nature of the outputs. In a market, we argue that the main focus must be on the output which is the subject of exchange. However, as Ouchi argues, the main issue for a market is having the information which is required to facilitate exchange and for the norm of reciprocity to prevail. In essence this requires information about prices. Where there is neither an ability to measure outputs nor to specify behaviour through a knowledge of the transaction process then the clan becomes a means to organise because it co-ordinates through ritual and shared norms and values. The informational requirements of the clan are held within the shared norms and values and are not concerned with issues of pricing.

Ouchi and Williamson both recognised that the categorisations they offered were not necessarily neat ones. Ouchi in particular recognised that all elements of control would be found in all organisations and we are anxious to emphasise their agreement with this. However, we argue that the changes in the public sector have been ones which have sought to change the balance of control away from more hierarchical and clan type controls and toward a market-based approach. If controls are to move from hierarchical and bureaucratic ones towards a more market-oriented approach then there are certain requirements which have to be met. In particular, the ability to measure outputs and to provide a price for the outputs is essential. Our argument is that 'accounting logic' is influential in promoting this shift in approach to control and that accounting as it is currently practised provides the technology for operationalising it. The particular implications of this for professionals will be discussed after the next section of the chapter explores the issue of accounting and 'accounting logic'.

THE NATURE OF 'ACCOUNTING LOGIC' AND ACCOUNTING

There is a general need for us to provide some account of our behaviour to others which can be encompassed by the notion of accountability. We would argue that accountability has been 'captured' by a particular approach which we call 'accounting logic'. 'Accounting logic' is a general approach built on two assumptions:

1 That any activity needs to be evaluated in terms of some measurable outputs achieved and the value added in the course of any activity.
2 That it is possible to undertake this evaluation in and through the financial resources actually used or received.

Thus, a central element of this mode of thinking is the view that it is possible to quantify outputs and outcomes and link them to financial inputs. 'Accounting logic' we see as pervasive and extensive and something which imbues society and is not simply related to accounting as it is practised by, for example, the large professional firms. It is a mode of thought which, if operated in full, requires that relationships have to be reflected in financial terms and the danger is that the structure of relationships could be changed to allow this type of quantification.[1] It is in some respects similar to the notion of economic reason although it differs in that it has the technology to operationalise these assumptions in accounting as it is currently practised, which we shall call *conventional accounting*, which utilises the assumptions of duality through double entry book-keeping.

'Accounting logic' is, therefore, particularly powerful because of the societal impact that it has. Following Gallhofer and Haslam (1991) we would argue that 'accounting logic' and its technology of conventional accounting have an aura of factual representation which promotes a general perception that the information which it produces is 'neutral, objective, independent and fair' (Gallhofer and Haslam, 1991: 495). More than that it is a public language which creates visibilities and downplays as unimportant anything not made visible (Broadbent, 1995). We would further argue that it is informed by a particular value set which emphasises those values typically associated with the socially constructed male stereotype (we should emphasise we do not see these as being essential elements of the biological male). Thus, the 'hard' values of reason, logic and material provision are emphasised at the expense of the 'softer' values of experience, intuition and nurturing. In the sense that conventional accounting as it is practised and 'accounting logic' do act to sustain and promote a particular set of values it can be argued that they are ideologically driven. This point will be developed more in the final section of the chapter. However, we see the ascendancy of the two as related to what has been seen as a societal rationalisation process which inevitably leads to a 'spread of countings and accountings' (Meyer, 1986: 347). This process itself also emphasises notions of standardisation and a search for common measurable yardsticks which aid that standardisation process and is accompanied by both monetarisation and a need for sophisticated exchange processes. It can also be seen as a manifestation of a Benthamite move from direct behaviour control to a more indirect form of constraint over people's behaviour (Gallhofer and Haslam, 1994a, 1994b).

Conventional accounting is far more than simply book-keeping, it comprises a whole technology of income and worth measurement. Much has been written about the nature of conventional accounting and there are those who see the activity as a technical practice (see the many textbooks on the subject); others see it much more as socially constructed (Tinker, 1985) and there are those who see it as socially constructing (Hines, 1988).

The American Accounting Association defined accounting as:

the process of identifying, measuring and communicating economic information to permit informed judgements and decisions by the users of the information

(American Accounting Association, 1966: 1)

It is possible to argue that this is a rather 'bland' and neutral description which gives a good sense of conventional accounting and how professional accountants would characterise their work. In particular, three elements might be highlighted, that we are dealing with a measurement system, that what is measured relates to the finances of definable entities and that it is intended as a means of communication of economic information to aid decisions. These characteristics are all commensurate with the underlying approach of 'accounting logic', especially in the desire to measure and communicate economic information. However, they also deal with the ideas of communication for decision making and we would argue that this is more in keeping with the overall need for accountability. Thus, it should be possible to provide accountability by focusing on the notion of information for decision making in a sense which is broader and in which the economic does not necessarily comprise the only element – this would demand a different approach to accounting (Broadbent and Laughlin, 1994). This does not mean that those undertaking activities will not be called to account for themselves, but that the nature of their accounting and accountability will be rather different to that which is provided by 'accounting logic' and conventional accounting.

In summary we would argue that there are four elements which we can distinguish; accountability, 'accounting logic', conventional accounting and accounting as it could be. We have a need for accountability, which we see as currently being given wide expression through 'accounting logic', a worldview in which a focus on measurement of activity and outputs in financial terms is legitimated and central. In conventional accounting we have a technology which operationalises this approach; in one sense conventional accounting is the 'ideal type' of accounting logic. The elements of quantification of outputs and emphasis on finances are ones which are essential if we are to operate a market-based approach to control in which there is a need to measure activity outputs and to attach prices to them to facilitate exchange. Thus, 'accounting logic', conventional accounting and market-based controls are all approaches which promote, enable and are logically consistent with each other. We would argue that accountability should not necessarily be equated with 'accounting logic', thus leading to conventional accounting, and that a broader view of information for decision making which is not economically focused could be adopted. The next strand in the argument is to look at why any of this is of relevance in a discussion about the professions.

THE NATURE OF PROFESSIONS

There are many conceptualisations of the notion of professions and some wide disagreements. One main axis of debate focuses on the extent to which it can be said that professions are characterised by certain identifiable traits or whether instead they are simply monopolies which control particular occupations. Our argument does not deny that there might be elements of a monopoly of competence (Larson, 1977) around the tasks which come under the control of certain professional groupings. It does not deny that professional groups will engage in attempts at closure around their area of activity (Witz, 1992). Despite this we accept that there is also some level of tacit knowledge (Polanyi, 1962, 1967; Nelson and Winter, 1982) which is needed by professionals in order to carry out their tasks successfully. The work of Jamous and Peloille (1970), which differentiates between indetermination and technicality, characterising professions by the high ratio of indetermination to technicality (I/T ratio), highlights the notion of tacit knowledge in a rather different fashion. Not all those activities which see themselves as professions can be seen to conform to this pattern (Dietrich and Roberts, 1995). However, we would argue that the professions in health and education, which are subject to legislative changes moving their mode of control, are ones in which the I/T ratio is relatively high.

If the professions with which we are concerned are ones which are characterised by the possession of high degrees of tacit knowledge or with a relatively high I/T ratio then it follows that the ability to define the nature of the transformation process is limited and that the definition of the outputs of the activity is also potentially problematic (as highlighted by Dietrich and Roberts in chapter 2 of this volume). In essence this should, using the Ouchi framework, render these tasks as unsuitable for both market and hierarchical controls and more relevant to *clan* aproaches to control. This problematic is one which is also reflected in the critique of economic reason developed by Gorz (1989) who argued that economic rationality was appropriate where activities had five characteristics: they created use values; for exchange as commodities; in the public sphere; in a measurable amount of time and at as high a level of productivity as possible. The caring professions fail on the last of these criteria to be suitable for the application of economic reason. Gorz sees alongside the provision of the service, a gift relationship from the carer which cannot be encompassed by maximisation of outputs, indeed he notes that the efficiency of carers might be in inverse proportion to their visible quantitative output (p.143).

The theoretical critique is reflected empirically. Our own longitudinal work in both schools and GP practices (substantiated by the views expressed in chapters 5 and 6 of this volume) suggests that those who work in the areas of medicine and education are very sceptical about the ability of the systems which have been created to encapsulate the entirety of their activities into the output indicators which are being used. If this is correct it follows that an approach based on output measurement, is at best, likely to measure only part of the activity of the group concerned. Another scenario is that the attempt to define and control through output measures may in fact lead to change in the nature of the activity. This can be argued to be the case in the recent legislation and the next section of the chapter will explore in more detail the nature of the changes which have been attempted as well as the responses to the changes. This is a precursor to the final discussion which seeks to evaluate the changes.

CHANGE IN THE PUBLIC SECTOR: CONTROLLING THE PROFESSIONAL

The examples which we shall use in this chapter are ones which are taken from the areas of education and GP practices in the UK, areas in which we have done longitudinal qualitative research. The aim of this section of the chapter will be to show the detail and the intention of the changes as well as the actuality of their implementation. The extent to which they accord with the claim that they move to a market approach to control will be highlighted.

Education

The Education Reform Act (DES, 1988) (ERA) was a key instrument in changing the administration of our education system in the UK. It provided two building blocks which have changed the manner in which education in schools is administered and delivered. Thus, it impacted both on management and teaching and the linkages between the two cemented to amplify the effect of the legislation. The first of these changes was a direct challenge to the professional core of teaching and sought to provide a control over what was actually taught. The core of the curriculum, which had never been formally specified, was defined in the National Curriculum (NC). The aim of the NC was to ensure that pupils in school studied a prescribed range of topics and subjects and that their proficiency in these areas was recorded and tested through a series of national examinations, called Standard Attainment Tests (SATs). Previously, although examination boards provided curricula for the subjects they examined, there had been a possibility for teachers to provide a curriculum which was specified through the professional and bureaucratic structures of the department in which they worked, the school and the policies of the Local Educational Authority. The NC and the recording and testing which accompanied it were widely criticised by the profession for both the lack of discretion over

41

content and the bureaucracy which the testing and accountability processes brought. Many different attainment targets were specified and pupils' ability in reaching the targets had to be recorded on an individual basis. The administering of SATs was also claimed to be time consuming and to provide information which teachers would routinely have available through their normal classroom activity. In essence the recording and testing were seen as ways of formally setting out information which a teacher already knew and taking away professional discretion. It was, perhaps, also an undermining of the trust to which professionals felt themselves entitled. In the light of the continued resistance to the SATs some changes to the NC were introduced following work by Sir Ron Dearing. Despite this the NC remains a control over professional activity and in this respect is, arguably, a clear move from a professional, clan type control. Although it cannot be seen on its own as a movement toward market-based controls, it can be argued to be a first step to puttting in place a necessary prerequisite to the market in that it attempts to provide a consistent output measure (league tables of examination results) based on the 'standard' input of the NC.

The NC was responsible for defining the core of teachers' work in the classroom and although some re-definition has been forced through, SATs are still in existence and the results of these along with the results of the national public examinations, GCSE and A-Levels, form a crucial link to the changed management arrangements ERA introduced. These included Local Management of Schools (LMS) in which budget responsibility has been delegated to individual schools. The market approach to control has been developed through a resource flow to schools which is largely based on the number of pupils, weighted for their age. What this means is that to receive resources a school has to attract pupils. The pupil numbers attracted must generate sufficient funds to employ enough staff to teach the specified areas of the NC. The market approach has been introduced through a relaxation of the right of the LEA to specify the school a child must attend and through a promotion of the notion of parental choice. The Parents Charter states:

> Your choice of school directly affects that school's budget – every extra pupil means extra money for the school. So your right to choose will encourage schools to aim for the highest possible standards.
>
> (DES, 1991: 14)

The choice of school is assumed to be made by the parent in the light of information about schools which will include their place in a national league table of examination results. The visibility of examination results is therefore seen as an important plank of making the 'market' work.

Longitudinal work with four schools in a northern LEA, alongside less intensive qualitative work with a further 24 schools in three other

LEAs (Broadbent, 1995; Broadbent, Laughlin and Willig-Atherton, 1994; Laughlin, Broadbent, Shearn and Willig-Atherton, 1994), suggests that there is a great deal of resentment about the intrusion of the NC and the introduction of league tables of examination results. The latter are not seen as able to measure everything a school 'really does' and there is some apprehension about their impact on the activities of schools in the long term. In making some aspects of the work of schools visible, there is a danger that other aspects which cannot be made visible will be down-graded (Broadbent, 1995). However, the visibility of outputs is essential to the operation of a market-based approach to control and to the move away from 'clan' approaches to control.

The fact that the changes have been imposed should not be taken to suggest that there has been no resistance to them. We have already noted that there was some resistance to the bureaucracy imposed by the SATs which was recognised and led to their change. Our empirical work has also shown that there has been some resistance to the management changes in that their impact has been limited to a small 'absorbing group' who have soaked up the changes with the stated intention of stopping their impingement on the main activities of the school – that of the educational processes. This has led to the involvement of senior teachers in management rather than educational processes and there is perceived to be a danger that the educational aspects might become de-centred as these managers become more closely involved in generic management tasks rather than educational issues. The recent suggestion by The Sec-retary of State for Education and Employment, Gillian Shephard, at the Conservative Party Conference in October 1995, that headteachers should take examinations dealing with such issues as personnel and budgeting emphasises the nature of the changing role of headteachers. The possible interface of professional 'clan' type controls with a managerial approach in a school environment remains to develop, but the definition of the curriculum along with the measurement of particular outcomes of the teaching process suggests that there is little sympathy with the con-tinuation of clan type approaches.

General Medical Practice

The changes which have impacted on General Practice include both the change to the GP Contract with the Family Health Services Authority and also the introduction of Fundholding. Our research has been centrally concerned with the introduction of changes to the GP contract and this will be the central focus of this section of the chapter.

The GP contract regulates the services which GPs provide to patients for which they are paid by the government via the Health Authorities. The contract revision which was implemented in April 1990, with a further revision in 1993, changed the basis on which GPs were remunerated. Previously the system had been one in which, whilst being paid a capitation fee for the patients on their list, GPs also received remuneration for other services they provided as and when those services were given. Thus, there was a type of 'piece rate' system in which doctors were paid for what they decided they had to do. The 1990 contract revision, for the first time, defined what doctors had to provide in order to receive their capitation payments. Thus, the hours a GP should be available were defined and the provision of a Practice Leaflet detailing services was demanded, as was the need to offer medicals for patients over 75 years of age or those patients who had not visited their GP for the past three years. Moreover the payments for additional services were considerably changed, some like the new patient medical continued to be paid for as they were completed. However, a range of other services would now only be paid for if 'targets' were achieved. These targets related to immunisations and to cervical cytology, and the logic of the scheme was that individual procedures were of no worth until the desired target was reached. Along with this, payments were to be made for the provision of Health Promotion Clinics and Disease Maintenance clinics, payment, again, being made when the attendance reached a target, in this case ten patients attending. The second revision of the contract has changed this slightly by abolishing the payments for clinics, but instead Health Promotion bandings have been implemented in which practices have to demonstrate the broader strategies they are taking to promote health within their patient population. This requires the collection of data about the patient population as well as the demonstration of strategies to meet patient need.

The implication of the changes was that if GPs were to maintain their income levels they now not only had to do what they thought appropriate as regards each particular patient but also had to ensure they achieved the appropriate target to trigger payment. The logic behind the payment system was that GPs were to be provided with a carrot (or a stick, depending on how the changes in remuneration were perceived) to carry out particular services. However, the services that GPs have been required to provide are not ones with which they are totally in agreement (Broadbent, 1994). Because of this, GPs are resentful that, in order to maintain income levels, they have to do things which are seen as inappropriate for their direct involvement (as Eve and Hodgkin discuss in a broader fashion in chapter 5 of this volume). Therefore, they have developed mechanisms to pass the tasks to others who they see as more equipped to deal with them. Practice Nurses have been employed to deal with the health promotion aspects of the Contract, and Practice Managers have been employed to deal with the attendant administration. The situation is similar to that in the schools with a small 'absorbing group' taking on the main burden of the changes to ensure that core general practice remains unaffected.

44

Education and Health: An Overview.

In both these cases the recent legislation has been concerned with the notion of specifying the tasks that teachers and GPs have to undertake. Moreover, they have specified the content of the activities in some detail and have an intention to take away discretion from the professionals concerned. They have done this by seeking to define outputs and link financial rewards to these outcomes and in this they are representative of 'accounting logic'. The detail of the legislation which has been implemented shows the difficulty in defining outputs and outcomes and that it is difficult to make direct linkages between the outputs and outcomes defined and the finances used. In the case of schools, the linkage is indirect, through parental choice guided supposedly by the informational content in the examination league tables. With GPs this is undertaken more overtly by the idea of payment for providing the desired services. In defining the nature of the services required there is a sense in which professional discretion to provide what is needed for the individual client (pupil or patient) is undermined. In this way the balance of control of the professional has been moved away from a clan approach where the professional norms and values and regulations guided the behaviour of the professionals concerned. Whilst the rhetoric which surrounds the various pieces of legislation extols the virtues of the market, the extent to which the controls are market-based or might be seen as more hierarchical remains unclear. What is clear is that in order for the balance of controls to move towards either of these approaches some specification of outputs is necessary.

IMPLICATIONS

The legislation which has been introduced has sought to place a much greater emphasis on the measurement of outputs and outcomes and make linkages between these and finances. In doing so it has implemented the notion of 'accounting logic' which emphasises the evaluation of activities both in terms of measurable outputs and through the lens of financial resources. Implementing this type of logic means that the controls which are exercised will be ones which also emphasise this approach and this has implications for professionals. Professionals, it can be argued, have been characterised by an ability to control their own spheres of activity. In that respect they have had great discretion over their tasks and this has sometimes led to criticism. The control structures which have developed are ones which have made them accountable to each other for the adherence to professional standards and norms. The definition of outputs has not been seen as possible to any great extent and the process of professional judgement is not seen as amenable to quantification and to detailed definition. For this reason Ouchi (1977, 1980) differentiated the notion of clan control which he saw as appropriate in circumstances where the outputs could not be defined and in which the transformation process was ill understood.

In implementing 'accounting logic' the rhetoric has been that of seeking the efficiency provided by the market. However, there is also evidence of more hierarchical control also being implemented. Market-based controls and hierarchical controls both require a defined output and some codification of the transformation process. Market-based controls also require that the output be expressed in financial terms (i.e. a price) so that exchange can be implemented. It follows that any attempt to move to these modes of control will affect the nature of professional work which is governed by them if these tenets are applied.

Perhaps, therefore, we might see the use of a market-based control as the 'best fit' approach for those whose desired approach is one seeking to adopt and implement 'accounting logic'. This is because it requires the expression of outputs in *financial* terms and so allows conventional accounting to come formally to the fore. Because it places so much emphasis on the notion of measurable outputs the use of this approach has to define outputs. What we see in the examples provided above are attempts to define outputs for various areas of professional work (for example, examination results for teachers, health promotion activities for GPs). However, we also see some attempt to define the transformation process. The definition of the curriculum and the specification of the health promotion activities of teachers and doctors also indicate that the government is not willing to trust to the market alone and that in fact they are seeking more than market control. The conclusion from this logic is that they wish to exercise a more hierarchical control over the professionals involved. This may be driven by the thinking that 'accounting logic' provides. An alternative is that the desire to control the professionals is driving the application of 'accounting logic' in this particular situation.

Professionals are very sceptical of the possibility that the output measures can actually capture the essence of all they are 'about' as professionals. Neither would they see the possibility of specifying their activities as feasible, because of the tacit nature of the knowledge base. Hence the changes are seen as ones which are clearly seeking to impose the interests of one group over another and as such they are seen to be ideologically motivated. The changes are ones which are seen as seeking to make visible certain aspects of professional activity simply to provide a means of control. The danger in this is that the areas which are given visibility and which are controlled might well undermine the other aspects of the tasks which are at the same time rendered invisible. In this way the whole nature of the professional activities could be changed. This may not necessarily be a bad thing as one desire is to provide accountabilities on the professionals concerned. However, we would argue that the debate about whether this is the case has not been developed. The work we have undertaken with teachers and GPs suggests that their efforts have been taken up with attempts to limit the impact of the initiatives which they see as damaging to their professional aims.

This does not mean that we would not wish to see professionals made accountable for their actions and activities. However, we would argue that the rendering accountable of those involved in professional activities should not necessarily be a process informed by 'accounting logic' and the technology of accounting as it presently exists. We would seek to find an accountability mechanism which was developed in a forum in which professionals, as well as those using their services in a broad sense, came together to develop meaningful accountabilities – see Broadbent and Laughlin (1994) for some initial thoughts on the design of such a framework.

The question of why seek to change the mode of control to a market base also needs to be considered. Above we have argued that this provides, perhaps, the clearest expression of 'accounting logic' – where the technology of conventional accounting can be fully operationalised. Despite this, the rhetoric of the market is not fully expressed in the initiatives. If we follow the logic of Williamson (1975) and his view of transaction costs then some indication of why this might be can be suggested. What we have is a situation in which there are long-term relationships and the skills and assets of health and education are ones which are fairly specific and not easily transferred to other situations. This would suggest that a hierarchical relationship would be formed and that the market would be inappropriate. Indeed, the changes have increased the hierarchical controls on the professionals concerned. This again suggests that the desire to control is paramount and that the claim for moving to market-based control is ideological.

In conclusion we would argue that it remains questionable as to whether the move from clan control has favoured hierarchical or market approaches to control. What is clear is that there has been a move to control professionals through the imposition of legislation informed by 'accounting logic'. Our plea would be that there be some broader evaluation of the changes (Laughlin and Broadbent, 1995a, 1995b) and that this should include consideration of the imposition of accountabilities which are meaningful to the professionals themselves as well as to those for whom they provide their services, both individually and as members of a wider society.

NOTES

1 The final section will show how this is not always possible and how 'accounting logic' must be subverted from its pure form in order to operationalise it in the public sector.

REFERENCES

American Accounting Association Committee to Prepare a Statement of Basic Accounting Theory (1966) *A Statement of Basic Accounting Theory,* Evanston: American Accounting Association.

Broadbent, J. (1994) 'Practice Managers and Practice Nurses: Gatekeepers and Handmaidens? A consideration of the effects of the new General Practitioners contract', *Sheffield University Management School Discussion Paper,* 94, 19.

Broadbent, J. (1995) 'The values of accounting and education: Some implications of the creation of visibilities and invisibilities in schools', *Advances in Public Interest Accounting,* 6: 69–89.

Broadbent, J. and Laughlin, R. (1994) 'Moving towards an accounting that will be enabling: Accounting, Habermas and issues of gender', *Proceedings of the Fourth Interdisciplinary Perspectives on Accounting Conference,* University of Manchester, July 1994: 1.3.1–1.3.18.

Broadbent, J., Laughlin, R. and Willig-Atherton, H. (1994) 'Financial controls and schools: Accounting in "Public" and "Private" spheres', *The British Accounting Review,* 26, 3: 255–79.

Coase, R.H. (1937) 'The nature of the firm', *Economica,* November: 386–405.

Department of Education and Science (1988) Circular 7/88, *Education Reform Act: Local Management of Schools,* London: DES.

Department of Education and Science (1991) *The Parents Charter: You and Your Child's Education,* London: DES.

Dietrich, M. and Roberts, J. (1995) 'Economics and the professions: The limits of free markets', Political Economy Working Papers, 4, PERC, University of Sheffield.

Gallhofer, S. and Haslam, J. (1991) 'The aura of accounting in the context of a crisis: Germany and the First World War', *Accounting, Organizations and Society,* 16, 5/6: 487–520.

Gallhofer, S. and Haslam, J. (1994a) 'Accounting and the Benthams: Accounting as negation', *Accounting, Business and Financial History,* 4, 2: 239–74.

Gallhofer, S. and Haslam, J. (1994b) 'Accounting and the Benthams: Or accounting's potentialities', *Accounting, Business and Financial History,* 4, 3: 431–60.

Gorz, A. (1989) *Critique of Economic Reason,* translated by Handyside, G. and Turner, C., London: Verso.

Hines, R.D. (1988) 'Financial accounting: In communicating reality, we construct reality', *Accounting, Organizations and Society,* 13, 3: 251–61.

Jamous, H. and Peloille, B. (1970) 'Changes in the French university hospital system', in J.A. Jackson (ed.) *Professions and Professionalization,* Cambridge: Cambridge University Press.

Larson, M.S. (1977) *The Rise of Professionalism: A Sociological Analysis,* Berkeley: University of California Press.

Laughlin, R. and Broadbent, J. (1995a) 'Evaluating the "New Public Management" reforms in the UK: A constitutional possibility?', Working Paper, University of Essex.

Laughlin, R. and Broadbent, J. (1995b) 'Redesigning fourth generation evaluation: An evaluation model for the public sector reforms in the UK?', Working Paper, University of Essex.

Laughlin, R., Broadbent, J., Shearn, D. and Willig-Atherton, H. (1994) 'Absorbing LMS: The coping mechanism of a small group', *Accounting, Auditing and Accountability* 7, 1: 59–85.

Meyer, J.W. (1986) 'Social environments and organizational accounting', *Accounting, Organizations and Society,* 11, 4: 345–56.

Nelson, R.R. and Winter, S.G. (1982) *An Evolutionary Theory of Economic Change,* Boston: Harvard University Press.

Ouchi, W. G. (1977) 'A conceptual framework for the design of organisational control mechanisms', *Management Science,* 25, 9: 833–48.

Ouchi, W.G. (1980) 'Markets, bureaucracies and clans', *Administrative Science Quarterly,* 25, 1: 129–41.

Polanyi, M. (1962) *Personal Knowledge: Towards a Post-Critical Philosophy,* London: Harper & Row.

Polanyi, M. (1967) *The Tacit Dimension,* London: Routledge & Kegan Paul.

Tinker, T. (1985) *Paper Prophets: A Social Critique of Accounting,* Eastbourne: Holt, Rinehart & Winston.

Williamson, O.E. (1975) *Market and Hierarchies: Analysis and Antitrust Implications,* New York: Free Press.

Witz, A. (1992), *Professions and Patriarchy,* London: Routledge.

4

LEADING PROFESSIONALS
Towards new concepts of professionalism
Robin Middlehurst and Tom Kennie

INTRODUCTION

This chapter explores change in the world of professionals and its impact on concepts of professionalism and professional practice in different locations, in particular contrasting the situation of the private sector professional with that of the individual in the multi-professional world of higher education – an example of the public sector. We begin by considering the changing nature of professional groups in society and concepts of professionalism which are associated with the activities of these groups. A discussion follows of some key environmental changes and their impact on professionals, particularly on their practice, their concepts of professionalism and on the nature of their professional organisations. The final sections of the chapter consider the role and value of leadership within a professional context, arguing that it is an increasingly important part of professional practice and needs to be deployed in the development of new concepts of professionalism which can extend beyond present boundaries.

THE GROWTH OF 'PROFESSIONALS'

The term 'professional' is neither uncontentious nor static. It is used to describe particular groups in society, but who is included in these groups varies over time and culture. It can also be used to denote the characteristics expected of the members of these groups, and emphasis is not always placed on the same characteristics. Various approaches have been adopted to define the essence of what might be seen to constitute 'professionalism', some relying on a description of the traits professional tasks might be seen to comprise (Jamous and Peloille, 1970); others have seen professionalism as more akin to a monopoly of competence (Larson, 1977). This chapter will not debate the nature of how we might define professionalism, *per se*, but will instead concentrate upon the growth and changing nature of those who identify themselves as professionals or are broadly categorised as such, societally.

A recent report by Watkins and his colleagues (1992) is helpful in identifying changes in groupings of professionals over time. Five groups of professionals are identified in the UK, developing from the sixteenth century:

- pre-industrial (1500): divinity, medicine, law;
- industrial (1800) (agricultural to industrial revolutions): engineers, chemists, accountants;
- welfare state (1900–1948): teachers, social workers;
- enterprise (1980s): business and management specialists;
- knowledge workers (1900s): information, communications and media specialists.

The authors note the blurring of distinctions between groups in response to wider socio-economic changes, for example, professional specialists taking on managerial functions and managers themselves becoming more specialised; advances in technology which make it easier for professionals and managers to delegate to technician and assistant professionals; and the development of multi-disciplinary practices. Whilst this framework might be challenged in various ways, it nevertheless provides a feel for the extension of the description 'professional' as well as indicating the changing nature of what is described by the term. Wilson (1991) suggests that in the period up to the year 2000 'professional' and 'associate professional' roles in the UK economy will increase by 21 per cent and 16 per cent respectively, whilst during the same period, jobs in manufacturing will decline by a further 10 per cent. The widening range of employment groups now regarded as 'professional' may in time reduce the exclusiveness associated with the term professional, this in turn offers the potential for developing some positive characteristics associated with being 'a professional'.

CONCEPTS OF PROFESSIONALISM

To some extent, the development of professional groups can be tracked by observing the establishment of representative professional bodies. These bodies, in offering membership within a 'club', have certain expectations of their members which reflect the more general characteristics claimed by professionals in addition to the specific requirements of each club. Some general characteristics include:

- a claim to represent, to have a level of mastery over, and to practise a particular discipline, skill, vocation or 'calling';
- advanced learning, usually represented by higher education qualifications (showing an ability to learn and amass knowledge);
- high level intellectual skills (showing an ability to grasp new events quickly and to respond effectively);

- independence and discretion within the working context (showing allegiance to an ethical framework and often to specific codes of practice which govern relationships between the profession, the professional, his/her clients and the wider society.

Professionals seek to build notions of professionalism on these characteristics in order to develop their legitimacy. In doing so they also use a rhetoric which claims many of the following features and involves a range of values, attitudes and behaviours:

- technical and theoretical expertise and the authority and status flowing from such expert and highly valued knowledge, understanding and skill;
- the establishment and the exercise of trust as a basis for professional relationships (with clients and between professionals);
- adherence to particular standards and professional ethics often, but not always, represented by the granting of a licence to practise;
- independence, autonomy and discretion;
- specific attitudes towards work, clients and peers involving dedication, reliability, flexibility and creativity in relation to the 'unknown'.

These features of professionalism are fluid and contested (Jarvis, 1983; Downie, 1990; Barnett, 1994) and periods of change bring the areas of contention into sharp relief; the elements are equally subject to fluctuations and differences across time, culture and discipline. One way of negotiating how we might focus on this changing nature is to consider two dimensions: what professionals do and the way in which they do it (professional practice) and the nature of the relationship between professionals and clients (professional relationships). Highlighting the interlinkage between these two elements illustrates the need to be aware of the effects of changes in the different links. How we view these elements will also depend on the perspective taken (for example, client, professional, professional body, professional organisation, society). For example, clients will be interested in the nature and quality of the service received as an aspect of what they pay for and seek from 'professionalism'; and society is likely to be interested in the conception, boundaries and costs of professionalism as part of deeper issues concerning the authority, legitimacy and accountability of professionals. The argument we seek to put forward is that there has been a great deal of change in these linkages in recent times. The late twentieth century has been characterised as a period of radical change when incremental shifts in economic, technological, political and social arenas have both converged and accelerated. The impact of such changes among professionals has been felt as a questioning of all aspects of professionalism; the value and status to be placed on professional knowledge and competence; the balance between implicit trust and explicit accountability between professionals and clients; the appropriate standards governing professional practice and relationships; the degree of independence and autonomy of professionals; and the means of developing and maintaining appropriate professional attitudes and behaviours. A further impact has been the development of differing modes of organising the provision of professional services in distinct locations.

THE PROFESSIONAL PROVIDING SERVICES IN THE PRIVATE SECTOR

Historically, the organisation of professional activities has developed from a 'sole practitioner' model in which the individual operated as a 'professional generalist', through a 'partnership' model where groups of professionals with complementary skills offer a range of specialist services, to increasingly complex multi-disciplinary professional service organisations. As these models of practice have developed, the balance of interest between professional autonomy and managerial accountability has also changed. For example, in small partnerships, all partners may share responsibility for elements of managing the practice, while in larger partnerships, the role of Managing Partner or Executive Committee has emerged as the locus of responsibility for management functions.

In some cases, particularly in larger multi-disciplinary practices, a separate role of Chief Executive may also be established. Occasionally, a role of this kind is filled by an individual who may not share the same professional background as that of the core business of the practice. It is rarer, however, for the individual not to share a career path which is closely associated with the culture and ethos of a related profession. In the largest professional service organisations, which in some instances have become limited companies or public limited companies (plc), the managerial and leadership decision-making authority may rest with a 'main board'. Nevertheless, while such organisations may share many of the features of corporate structures in other business sectors, they often retain a culture which reflects their partnership ethos and background; they often behave more as a 'public limited partnership' (plp), than a plc !

THE PROFESSIONAL IN THE PUBLIC SECTOR: THE CASE OF ACADEMIC PRACTICE

Academics often operate as individual entrepreneurs in the various fields of human knowledge, or as teams of entrepreneurs, pushing forward the boundaries of their subject and trading their knowledge and ideas. Typically, the pursuit of an academic career relies upon a high degree of personal initiative and intrinsic motivation, rewards and promotion being achieved through a process of peer judgment and recognition.

Until relatively recently in the UK, relationships with clients and stakeholders, whether students, research contractors and sponsors or government, have been based on a large measure of trust built on an acknowledgment of academic expertise and professionalism. Trust of this sort has also been accompanied by a degree of protection from the perceived rigours of the external world (particularly the structures, values and disciplines of the business environment). This kind of relationship between providers and knowledge creators on the one hand and the recipients or beneficiaries of knowledge on the other was gradually developed over many centuries. It was founded on the need for mastery and continued development of a field of knowledge; through a recognition of the intellectual space required for creativity and knowledge generation; by an acknowledgment of the existence and observation of a code of ethical standards governing academic practice (albeit a largely tacit code); and through an acceptance of the necessary role of universities as important contributors – and critics – of society.

In their internal organisation, this foundation of individual 'academic freedom' has been reflected in traditions of institutional autonomy (particularly in the UK). Higher education institutions have been based largely on democratic decision-making processes which have operated through consent, a form of internal self-government made possible by a network of committees and a widespread internalisation of common values and culture (although, as Becher (1989) has demonstrated, academic culture is in reality not monolithic, but fragmented into a number of disciplinary cultures. In the last quarter of the twentieth century this picture of individual freedom and institutional autonomy has been changing as relationships between knowledge, education, society and the economy have shifted (Barnett, 1994). The changing external environment has its impact on professionals in different spheres.

CHANGES AFFECTING PRIVATE SECTOR PROFESSIONAL PRACTICES AND PROFESSIONAL SERVICE ORGANISATIONS

Over the past decade a number of major changes have taken place in the external business environment within which many professional practices and professional service organisations operate. A summary of some of the major changes is provided in Table 4.1.

These changes can be seen partly as a consequence of an economic recession which is affecting many industrialised nations and the resulting competitive pressures which have affected all sectors of the UK business community. The changes are also, however, a response to a number of longer-term transformational influences which are reshaping the nature of the working environment.

Table 4.1 General environmental changes

From	To
1 Demand for services	1 Over-supply of providers
2 Wide range of suppliers (sole practitioners to large partnerships)	2 More limited range (niche players to large partnerships/PLCs)
3 Differentiation in terms of technical expertise	3 Differentiation in terms of quality and service
4 Short-term opportunism and client relationships	4 Longer-term accountability and partnership agreements
5 Advertising products/services to an undifferentiated market place	5 Marketing by understanding, uncovering and satisfying client needs
6 Professional as a highly regarded 'technical expert'	6 Professional as a technical adviser and one of a number of 'business consultants'

One of the key reasons for these significant changes in the working environment can be argued to be the growing impact of information technology. IT provides the capability to store, retrieve, analyse and communicate data in a manner which was not conceivable twenty years ago. Its impact is perhaps even more dramatic on the shape and design of organisations. One could argue that many businesses are changing their organisational structures to match more closely the characteristics of traditional professional practices, with their flat hierarchies and local 'partner' level decision making. In many other senses, however, the traditional professional practice is also changing. IT enables parts if not all of the technical expertise, previously the sole preserve of the professional, to be available to a much wider population. Team working, and sharing data, concepts and ideas through the medium of IT, is likely to become a much more powerful way for professionals to operate in the future.

The impact of a changing external environment on individuals is also producing a combination of short-term responses to the prevailing economic conditions and longer-term modifications to employment conditions and career development. A summary of some of the most significant changes at an individual level is illustrated in Table 4.2.

Table 4.2 Some of the principal changes affecting professionals: 1985–1995

From	To
1 Expectation of a 'job for life'	1 Reality – 'no job is safe'
2 Generally single employer (increasing specialisation)	2 Multiple employers (and potentially multiple careers)
3 Develop a single specialist skill	3 Adaptable and flexible – multiple skills required
4 Careers planned – vertical hierarchical promotion	4 Plan your own career – horizontal/lateral development

The trend from 'employment' to 'employability' in business has been a feature of professionals' career development. In the past, however, it was predominantly the domain of the senior professionals (partner level); it is now a concept of importance at every professional level as the nature of professional careers changes.

Traditionally, professional careers have developed by a process of increasing specialisation after an initial apprenticeship which gave a broad foundation of experience. The route to the higher levels of the professions relied upon evidence of a capability to handle increasingly complex professional or technical problems. Gradually, over the past five to ten years, other career routes have developed. We might differentiate two further career paths which involve either a broader 'professional generalist' approach or a 'managerial/business generalist' direction. In the former case, the role of the senior professional is more of a project manager, co-ordinating skills from a number of professional or multi-professional disciplines; alternatively, he or she may act as a 'general practitioner' dealing with a wide range of problems, usually at a less detailed level. The role of the senior professional as a business-generalist involves a significant proportion of time on business development and practice management matters, whilst retaining some direct work with clients. Increasingly, many 'specialist professionals' are also finding that they are being required to develop new business and managerial skills and this may lead to tensions as the balance shifts towards the professional as 'business winner' and 'manager'. We discuss this further in the final section.

CHANGES IN THE PUBLIC SECTOR: THE CASE OF THE HIGHER EDUCATION ENVIRONMENT

In the macro-environment of universities and colleges, economic shifts and technological developments have had as profound an impact on institutions as on professional service organisations. Innovations in information technology have both facilitated and made necessary changes in institutional management, in teaching and learning strategies and in the size, location and number of institutions. 'Outreach' approaches, distance learning, decentralised decision making and flexible patterns of working and studying have become widespread. Other scientific advances, such as controls over human conception, have also had a significant impact on employment patterns, family relationships and individual aspirations, enabling larger numbers of women, for example, to participate in and benefit from higher education and to enter the professions.

The economic recession which has affected western industrialised nations during the last decade has brought into question the level of public funds available for higher education while at the same time perceived links between wealth creation and education have fuelled demand for a more educated and highly skilled workforce. Political responses to these economic pressures have sought to encourage in UK institutions a greater emphasis on market values and practices in an effort to reduce dependence on state support, and have sought to exert greater leverage on the nature of internal activities, from management to the curriculum.

The demand for an educated and competent workforce comes as much from business as from government. While changes have taken place in higher education in the UK, for example in the development of more highly vocational courses, in the extension of access routes to higher education, in the growth of continuing education and in the overall expansion of higher education from approximately 15 per cent of the relevant age group in 1985 to over 30 per cent in 1995, educational changes outside higher education will also have a long-term impact on developments in the sector. These include the growth in training and education opportunities offered in the private sector and developments in vocational qualifications which focus on competencies learned and assessed in the workplace. Some of these trends are summarised in Table 4.3 below.

Table 4.3 Some of the principal changes in the operating environments of higher education institutions in the UK: 1985–1995

From	To
1 Limited access to HE	1 Wider access/increased availability of HE
2 Broadly homogeneous providers	2 Heterogeneous providers
3 Limited delivery modes	3 Variety of delivery modes
4 Academic autonomy	4 Accountability to stakeholders
5 Limited competition	5 Heightened competition and increased resource pressures

A changing external environment has affected institutions and individuals in the UK in different ways, but a number of general themes can be discerned. At institutional level, economic pressures have resulted in drives to increase efficiency (CVCP, 1985) and efforts to generate income from sources other than the state. External assessment mechanisms (for research and for teaching) have been introduced by the Funding Councils in order to assess value for money in the use of public funds and to distribute these funds selectively.

Responses to economic pressures to reduce and control costs, to generate income and to demonstrate value for money while at the same time seeking to expand higher education provision, have produced widespread internal restructuring. Management and delivery systems have been affected, consultative mechanisms have been altered, staff roles, responsibilities and terms of employment are changing, new quality assurance arrangements are being developed and there is a growing concern about the cumulative impact of all these changes on research, teaching, learning and the student experience of higher education.

The impact of change on individuals has been as great in higher education as in other 'professional' sectors. Some of the principal changes affecting academics are illustrated below.

Table 4.4 Some of the principal changes affecting university 'professionals': 1985–1995

From	To
1 Security of tenure	1 Fixed and short-term contracts
2 Emphasis on technical/professional skills	2 Emphasis on professional and management skills
3 Self-monitoring	3 External performance evaluation
4 Limited training and career development	4 Professional development emerging

Academic career paths are changing as much as those of other professionals. Where a traditional linear career route might have involved progression from lecturer through senior/principal lecturer to professor, a range of different tracks is now emerging. Teaching expertise is beginning to be separated from research expertise, so that parallel career tracks are possible; and in both cases, management and leadership skills are gaining prominence. Short-term contracts are common, particularly among researchers, and the nature of the teaching and research functions themselves are changing. For example, aspects of the teaching function may also now be carried out by librarians, laboratory technicians, or post-graduate assistants, while research is developing into a team or group activity even in the humanities, with groups sometimes spread across disciplines and countries. Periods of time spent in industry or other external contexts are not uncommon and senior posts may often be filled by applicants from outside higher education. The boundaries of role, technical expertise and organisational experience are becoming more permeable.

THE IMPACT OF CHANGE ON PROFESSIONALS

Impact on professionalism and professional activities

In the section above, some of the larger-scale changes affecting different groups of professionals have been outlined. In this section we look more closely at the impact of change on the activities of professionals and the ways in which these are causing shifts in notions of professionalism wherever they may be located. Despite the differing contexts there are some important commonalities.

Two related themes can be argued to have come to dominate professional activities in the past two decades: quality and accountability. 'Quality', often defined as fitness for purpose where purpose is determined in large part by the identification and satisfaction of customer requirements, is largely a response to competitive pressures in the economy. Defining one's practice, service or product in terms of 'better' quality than that produced by competitors has had an impact both on professional practice itself and on the process of managing the services delivered. These developments have been given a sharper edge by being linked to accountability, where accountability can be described as rendering an account of practice or service (and the quality of that practice/service) to third parties. In higher education, our example from the public sector, there are several identifiable groups of third parties including parents of students; employers and businesses; and government, as proxy for the tax-payer, society and the economy. In professional practice in the private sector, 'third parties' include professional and statutory bodies as regulators of practice on behalf of society, as well as government as proxy for the tax-payer.

Advances in technology have encouraged an explosion in the production and availability of information which is now accessible to a variety of audiences. As customers and sponsors alike have become better informed, they have become more demanding about the services delivered by professionals. Without developments in technology, many of the changes in professional practice, its organisation and delivery would not have been possible. Similarly, developments in quality management, such as the identification and satisfaction of customer requirements and the measurement and evaluation of performance (both part of the machinery of quality and accountability) could not have been furthered without technological advances.

The impact of these developments on notions of professionalism is already profound. If we refer to the characteristics of professionalism described earlier, a number of trends can be detected:

- technical and theoretical expertise is no longer sufficient to establish authority and status, continued professional development, management expertise and leadership capability are also needed;
- trust built on professional mystique is being replaced by trust built on transparency about the nature of professional competence, and accountability for professional services to both direct and indirect beneficiaries or sponsors;
- professional standards are being revisited and closely monitored in the light of changes in expectations about professional behaviour and client relationships;
- independence, autonomy and discretion are being challenged both by notions of quality and accountability and by new developments in

knowledge and technology which are shifting the boundary between routine and novel professional procedures and problems;

• traditional professional attitudes to work, clients and peers are still expected, but many of the developments described above are making them more difficult to achieve;

• a premium is being placed on a skill traditionally developed in higher education and required of professionals operating in a swiftly changing environment, i.e. professional 'critique' or challenging of the assumptions and processes underpinning professional practice.

These shifts in 'professionalism' call for a re-appraisal of professional values and ethics, professional education and training, the delivery of professional services and the evaluation of professional performance.

Organisational impact

The ways in which organisations are designed in order to carry out particular functions and to deliver particular services have changed over time. The nature of the changes and their impact on the interactions of organisational participants has been described in terms of different metaphors of organisational culture. Some prominent metaphors (Bensimon *et al.*, 1989; Morgan, 1986) are outlined below in order to draw out some of the characteristics of change in organisations of professionals:

A collegial perspective – where the organisation is viewed as a 'community' of practitioners within which decisions are reached by consensus and where the internal structure is based on seniority and professional expertise. Common codes of practice and ethical conduct provide cultural bonds which assist in integrating the interests and activities of the professionals. In higher education, this is an image often associated with collegiate universities, while in the professions such a perspective is usually linked to the 'learned society' aspects of the work of professional bodies in developing the knowledge base of the profession. The image is also relevant to some professional partnerships.

A political perspective – where diversity of activity and professional interest within the organisation is recognised as creating the potential either for conflict or for creative tension leading to successful organisational functioning. Mediation and negotiation between departments or key groups are often the levers for successful decision making. This cultural image recognises the need to balance, for example, the legitimate interests of academics and administrators, historians and physical scientists, or senior professionals and senior managers in private practices.

A bureaucratic perspective – where complexity of organisational activities is a central feature and where structure is seen as the key to co-ordination and control. A division of labour into functional units organised though hierarchical chains of command characterises this form of organisation. Within groupings of professionals, there is often a tension between the independence and professional autonomy of practitioners who desire minimal 'bureaucratic control' and managers' requirements for policies and structures which create consistency and encourage standardisation in day-to-day internal operating procedures and in the delivery of external services to clients.

An entrepreneurial perspective – where the organisation is viewed as a provider of products and services to a range of internal and external markets, its central features being those of a trading enterprise. The organisation (or collective entity) can be conceived as a series of developing and evolving organisms, dependent on the central system for 'nutrients' in the form of pump-priming finance, external marketing, etc. Another image would be of a central holding company with a series of semi-independent satellite/business units who buy services from the centre and sell services to the external world.

A learning organisation perspective – where the organisation is viewed as a flexible, self-correcting, learning system which is able to adapt to a changing external environment, through the operation of interactive processes and minimal managerial dictate. Information is widely available so that the evaluation of professional activities can be an on-going process managed by professionals at the point of delivery of services to clients. The image of the organisation as an open system, responding to and promoting changes in its external and internal environment, is also relevant to this perspective.

Each of these images provides an alternative view of some key characteristics of academic organisations, professional practices and professional service organisations. The richness of such organisations provides great strength and resilience, although this can also be manifested as resistance to change. Where different characteristics exist, and where perceptions of their importance for smooth organisational functioning differ in the same organisation, considerable tensions may emerge. Such tensions have increased, for example, at the interface between the 'management of academic activities' and the 'management of institutional activities' within higher education, and within professional practices / professional service organisations in the private sector at the interface between the 'management of professional activities' and the 'management of practice activities'. In recent restructuring exercises in both types of organisation, new internal organisational forms are emerging which attempt to resolve such tensions (Middlehurst and Kennie, 1995).

At a time of change, the dominance of particular organisational perspectives is likely to shift. Across many types of professional practice and organisation, the earlier prominence of collegial and bureaucratic perspectives is changing towards entrepreneurial and learning forms of organisation. However, it is often the case that organisational structures change faster than the values and behaviours of individual practitioners and it is here that leadership has an important role to play.

LEADERSHIP AND PROFESSIONALS IN A CHANGING CONTEXT

Leadership and change

Several authors have noted the relationship between change and leadership. Adair (1983) suggests that a changing context creates instability, uncertainty and a need for adaptation in individual roles and attitudes as well as organisational structures and cultures. Such turbulence creates both a psychological and a practical need for leadership. He also suggests, in common with Zaleznik (1977) and Bennis (1989), that those who are leaders will themselves initiate change, whether as a result of their own psycho-social make-up or as a result of the social and cultural expectations surrounding 'leadership'. Change and leadership are therefore closely linked: change creates the need for leadership and leaders are, or are perceived to be, initiators and drivers of change.

Kotter (1990) presents a slightly different picture, but the association between leadership and change is maintained. He suggests, first, that a distinction can be made between leadership and management. Leadership at senior levels encompasses the direction-setting, inspirational and motivational aspects necessary for effective organisational development, while management includes the planning, co-ordinating and financial capacities which enable a complex organisation to operate efficiently on a continuing basis. Leadership and management are therefore two necessary and complementary systems of action. Kotter then argues that leadership is required to effect or to cope with change, while management is needed to handle complexity within and around organisations.

An association between leadership and change helps to explain why there are calls for stronger leadership in universities and colleges and in professional service organisations at the present time; it also demonstrates a major purpose of leadership at organisational level, i.e. to effect changes in structure and culture which will enable the organisation to survive and develop.

Common understandings of leadership as 'a process of social influence which guides a group towards common goals' (Bryman, 1986) also imply that leadership is linked to movement and change. These associations highlight further purposes of organisational or group leadership which include: interpreting the external environment in relation to organisational mission, reputation and tradition; providing vision and direction for the organisation; creating new organisational frameworks and structures, roles and opportunities where necessary; taking and assessing risk to the organisation and attempting to position it in the market-place; aligning people with a new direction through consultation, communication, coalition-building and networking; representing the organisation, legally, politically and symbolically, and arbitrating between conflicting priorities (Middlehurst, 1993).

Leadership and the expectations of professionals

Adair (1983) has identified leadership as a function which addresses the needs which arise for those working in organisations, that is, the need to successfully achieve a task or tasks, the need to be linked together co-operatively and productively as a working group, and the need to achieve individual satisfaction and recognition for contributions to a shared enterprise. Bensimon *et al.* (1989) argue the case somewhat differently, although there are common elements. In their terms, effective leadership involves resource acquisition, goal achievement and constituent satisfaction, the last being particularly interesting since most professional organisations have a wide range of different constituencies which need to be satisfied. Often, these groups have conflicting priorities and interests (for example, the interests of providers and clients, academics and administrators, students and researchers). Leadership therefore often involves trade-offs, dilemmas, and 'the negotiation of ambiguities'.

As was discussed earlier, some of the key characteristics of professionals (whether academics in universities or professionals in private practices and PLCs) are their expectations of individual autonomy, effectively granted as a 'licence to practise' by their professional institution; their expertise (generally reflecting articulacy and intellectual standing); and their intrinsic motivation for 'self-actualisation' through worthwhile work, to use Maslow's term (1954). Loyalties exist towards a discipline or professional area as much as towards the employing organisation, and often a close relationship is anticipated and developed with clients. Lateral networks with clients and professional colleagues which extend outside the boundaries of the organisation are as important as internal networks. Indeed, because of high degrees of structural and managerial devolution to operating units in professional organisations (which have traditionally been present and are now being extended as a result of emphases on quality and accountability at the point of delivery of services), vertical and particularly horizontal relationships may be relatively weaker in these kind of organisations than in other more hierarchical arrangements. External lateral relationships can therefore often exert a stronger pull in terms of a professional's 'psychological contract' with his/her work than does the formal contract with the employing organisation. The impact of information technology on these lateral professional networks is likely to increase their relevance and importance.

Leadership in organisations of professionals must take into account the particular structural features of these kinds of organisation as well as their present context and circumstances, the characteristics of the relevant practitioners and the expectations of major stakeholders/clients. In essence, leadership is likely to be a political and intellectually complex activity in which interpreting, negotiating, building formal and informal networks, framing, signalling, challenging, guiding, wielding influence and providing direction are of central importance in creating an appropriate environment and climate for professional work. Leadership will involve developing both the harder structural aspects of the organisation as well as the softer aspects of values, purpose, meaning and culture and aligning them appropriately. The purpose of leadership in professional organisations, however, remains similar to its purpose in any organisation: making it happen, deciding and articulating what 'it' is, and taking people with you individually and corporately.

Distributed leadership

In our discussion, we have concentrated largely on organisational leadership. Clearly, leadership exists at many levels of the organisation (for example, at operational and team, as well as strategic levels) and outside the organisation at the level of government or regulatory agency. The need for leadership to be widely distributed, to be participative and to be perceived as a shared function is particularly relevant in professional organisations. Many individuals and groups will need to exercise initiative, take risks, be innovative and creative in their own spheres of activity as well as in the service of the whole enterprise. For example, in universities, it is possible to think in terms of educational leadership exercised within the wider society, academic leadership exercised in relation to teaching and research and administrative or managerial leadership exercised in relation to the effective functioning of a unit or organisation. In each case, leadership involves guiding by being creative, by detecting patterns, by articulating purpose and by fostering commitment to collective goals.

In professional practices it is also possible to describe leadership as an activity which exists in a widely distributed form. First, at one level there exists the need for professional leadership; the development of new thinking, or the reframing of existing thought in relation to a particular technical/professional issue. Second, there also exists the need for business and client leadership in developing new approaches to the market for professional services. And third, a practice of any size could not operate in a modern business context without managerial/administrative leadership to ensure the efficient and effective operation of the practice including the deployment and redeployment of resources to meet the peaks and

troughs of demand. The more strategic, visionary, direction-setting characteristics of leadership are likely to be exhibited in all three areas, perhaps
in contrast to more traditional organisations where this function is more
commonly associated solely with 'managerial/administrative' leadership.

NEW CONCEPTS OF PROFESSIONALISM

Benefits of professionalism

There are numerous benefits to society and economy of 'professionalism'
and of those activities commonly associated with professionals. For
example, professional skills supply necessary services and, if delivered at
a consistently high level, provide competitive advantage for the economy.
The granting of professional independence and discretion, particularly
when exercised with responsibility, dedication and creativity, is a significant economic benefit since it obviates the need for close, detailed and costly
supervision and monitoring of service delivery and overall performance.

However, as outlined above, professional autonomy is premised on
relationships of trust built on mutual respect between clients/sponsors
and professionals and belief in the value of professional services. Recent
emphases on quality and accountability for professional services suggest
that the basis of trust in professionals is changing, as discussed earlier.
Current regulatory manifestations threaten to undermine the economic
benefits of professionalism, as the costs in bureaucratic monitoring and
inspection and time spent in evaluating the performance of professionals,
by professionals, escalate. What is needed for the future is a re-estab-
lishment of notions of professionalism in which quality and accountability
are delivered as a matter of course to third parties, in ways which are
integrated into practice rather than being bureaucratic add-ons.

A further important benefit of professionalism lies in the scope for self-
generation and regeneration of professional knowledge and practice in the
light of change. Higher education plays an important part in this through
the initial development of critical faculties in undergraduate programmes,
and through research. Developing 'the reflective practitioner' (Schon, 1983;
1987) through continuing professional development both at work and
through further study should continue to focus on the skills of problem-
solving, critical evaluation and innovation which are essential features for
the survival and development of flexible and responsive practitioners.

The role of leadership and management

If concepts of professionalism are to be both redefined and extended more
widely within the working context, then the functions of leadership and
management will need to be drawn upon as levers for change and as

important components of a new professionalism. As we have suggested, a changing context increases the need for the exercise of leadership in order to redirect and reframe professional activities and behaviours and to re-assess professional values. An increasingly complex environment, in which accountability, value-for-money, and interdependence of professional services are key features, illustrates the parallel need for management skills and expertise. The development and exercise of leadership and management functions is becoming a necessary part of the portfolio of skills required of professionals. Some evolving roles for professionals illustrate the kinds of skills that are required for the future:

Client relationships – traditionally, the term 'client' referred only to those who received and paid for professional services. Increasingly, however, the concept of 'a client' is widening to include, for example, other groupings of professionals in their role as strategic partners or networked associates who supply services to one or more firms; professional associations who may lobby and influence third parties on a collective basis on behalf of individual practitioners as well as internal clients; and other internal professional colleagues who may cross-refer opportunities. In higher education, as we have already indicated, the concept of 'client' (or customer) includes not only students and institutional managers, but also other groups such as sponsors or professional bodies. Managing the relationships with multiple stakeholders, with their range of needs and interests, is a much more significant role than the traditional one of serving the needs of a single client.

People relationships – integrating the work of other professionals in order to provide efficient and effective professional services to clients requires a well managed internal working environment. Whether the task is building a research team or developing a modular scheme for the delivery of undergraduate programmes in higher education, or undertaking a strategic property review for a corporate client which requires the building of a team of professional surveyors and 'support' staff, there is a need to establish productive working relationships with others. Interpersonal skills such as leadership, team-building and negotiating are important aspects of professional roles.

Professional work – specific technical skills or a range of technical skills, remain an important part of the concept of 'a professional'. It is increasingly expected by clients, sponsors and the 'guardians' of the professions, the professional associations, that these skills will be updated, extended and developed further in new and creative ways, in a spirit of continuous learning and enterprise. Professionals need to be both entrepreneurs and intrapreneurs, developing their practice externally and their organisations internally in response to change.

Managing the practice/organisation – economic, social and technological changes in the environment in which professionals operate mean that more emphasis has to be placed on running the business. Acquiring, deploying and accounting for resources, co-ordinating activities and delivering customised services on time requires skills in 'practice management'. These skills may be developed early through experience in project and team management, but at the unit or organisational level, the breadth of vision, range of activities and pace of response are of a different order of magnitude.

This illustrates the changing balance of responsibilities and duties associated with a professional role. Traditionally, the main role and duty of a professional was to his/her primary (fee-paying) clients with management being construed largely in terms of 'office administration'. Increasingly, however, professionals are required to undertake a new balance of roles. In large practices or academic units the roles may be split, in small organisations an individual would expect to carry multiple roles. These will include responding to the needs of an increasingly sophisticated and educated client base; providing appropriate accountability and value for money in the services offered; and responding to the pressures of running a complex modern enterprise (for example, covering a range of practice management matters, from tax and accounting conventions, to personnel legislation and health and safety regulations). In a competitive environment, marketing individual expertise and collective professional services is also of paramount importance.

'A new professionalism' does not only require the development of a wider range of skills and an extended series of professional roles, but also requires the development of different attitudes and behaviours among professionals. Client service and client relationships require professionals to put the needs of their clients rather than the interests of their profession at the centre of their practice – for commercial *and* professional reasons. Quality in client services and relationships also has to be matched by quality in internal relationships and management systems so that the benefits of professionalism are consistently evident through client transactions at individual and organisational levels. Creating responsive professional organisations, peopled by creative, multi-skilled and enterprising professionals, requires imaginative and sensitive leadership which places value not only on financial performance, but also on ethical practice, investment in people, and the development of long-term partnerships with many different kinds of clients.

REFERENCES

Adair, J. (1983) *Effective Leadership*, London: Pan.
Barnett, R. (1994) *The Limits of Competence: Knowledge, Higher Education and Society*, Buckingham: SRHE/ Open University Press.

Becher, T. (1989) *Academic Tribes and Territories; Intellectual Enquiry and the Culture of Disciplines*, Milton Keynes: SRHE/ Open University Press.

Bennis, W. (1989) *On Becoming a Leader*, London: Hutchinson.

Bensimon, E., Neumann, A. and Birnbaum, R. (1989) *Making Sense of Administrative Leadership: The 'L' Word in Higher Education*, Washington, DC: ASHE/ERIC, Higher Education Report No. 1.

Bryman, A. (1986) *Leadership in Organisations*, London: Routledge & Kegan Paul.

CVCP (1985) *Report of the Steering Committee of Efficiency Studies in Universities*, London: CVCP.

Downie, R.S. (1990) 'Professions and professionalism', *Journal of Philosophy of Education*, 24, 2: 147–59.

Jamous, H. and Peloille, B. (1970) 'Changes in the French university hospital system', in J.A. Jackson (ed.) *Professions and Professionalization*, Cambridge: Cambridge University Press.

Jarvis, P. (1983) *Professional Education*, London: Croom Helm.

Larson, M.S. (1977) *The Rise of Professionalism: A Sociological Analysis*, Berkeley: University of California Press.

Kotter, J. (1990) *A Force for Change: How Leadership Differs from Management*, New York: Free Press.

Maslow, A.H. (1954) *Motivation and Personality*, New York: Harper & Row.

Middlehurst, R. (1993) *Leading Academics*, Buckingham: SRHE/Open University Press.

Middlehurst, R. and Kennie, T.J.M. (1995) 'Leadership and professionals: Comparative frameworks', *Tertiary Education and Management* 1, 2: 120–30 .

Morgan, G. (1986) *Images of organisation*, London: Sage.

Schon, D. A. (1983) *The Reflective Practitioner: How Professionals Think in Action*, London: Temple Smith.

Schon, D. (1987) *Educating the Reflective Practitioner: Towards a New Design for Teaching and Learning in the Professions*, San Francisco: Jossey-Bass.

Watkins, J., Drury, L. and Preddy, D. (1992) *From Evolution to Revolution: The Pressures on Professional Life in the 1990s*, Bristol: University of Bristol.

Wilson, R. A. (1991) *Review of the Economy and Employment (Occupational Assessment)*, Warwick: Institute of Employment Research, University of Warwick.

Zaleznik, A. (1977) 'Managers and leaders: Are they different?', *Harvard Business Review*, 55: 67–78.

5

PROFESSIONALISM AND MEDICINE

Rosalind Eve and Paul Hodgkin

The experience of working to someone else's prescription is seldom as satisfying as working to one's own. The price of calling the tune and making the professionals dance to it is that they usually do so only half-heartedly.

Raine and Willson (1993: 98)

INTRODUCTION

Medicine is undergoing an intense degree of change brought about by Government pressure to constrain the costs of health care, technological advances, an increasingly elderly population with the consequent rise of chronic disease and the information revolution. In addition, medicine is the only one of the traditional 'learned professions' which is also scientific and technologically based. All this means that medicine occupies a singular and interesting position amongst the professions.

This chapter first examines the particular pressures on medicine together with the consequent changes and challenges. Following this, we look at the ways in which the profession has tried to adapt its own ideology in order to cope and the responses of the system which have tended to increase accountability of the profession. Finally, we turn to the future and look at what wider cultural changes may bring to the medical profession of the next decades.

The chapter is written from a particular perspective. First, the authors are essentially practitioners in the system rather than observers of it. One of us is a general practitioner whilst the other has been involved in promoting and managing change within a large number of general practices within one city. What we have to say comes from trying to make sense of the rapidly changing world in which we have found ourselves and not from an academic or disinterested position. Second, we have worked in a particular context: the British National Health Service (NHS) and the intended and unintended consequences of the reforms implemented from 1989 onwards that have provided the changing backdrop to our experience of coping with change.

Professionalism is often defined as being a vocation in which professed knowledge is used in the affairs of others. We have used a more task-oriented definition:

A professional task is one which requires the exercise of discretion or initiative on behalf of another in a situation of complexity.

Thus according to this definition an experienced hairdresser assisting an uncertain client might exhibit more elements of professionalism than a doctor slavishly following a rigid protocol without regard to the individual circumstance of the patient or the wider context in which s/he works. We will return to the significance of this at the end of the chapter.

MEDICINE'S PARTICULARITY – WHAT'S SO SPECIAL ABOUT MEDICINE?

There are a number of things which make medicine special amongst the professions. These include:

• the huge amount of money which has been expended on biomedical research and technological development since the war. This has generated a much greater body of knowledge to be accommodated than that in say social work or accountancy. The rate at which this knowledge accumulates shows no sign of abating;
• its commitment to the notion that there is a single, definable version of the 'truth' which can be revealed by scientific, reductionist methods;
• a strong tradition of clinical freedom: that the interpretation of the truths revealed by biomedical science demands the exercise of an independent, professional discretion on behalf of patients;
• at some level medicine touches the certainty of death. This makes it of more universal interest than say teaching or the law. At the same time, the desire in all of us to believe that we can call on powerful forces to defer death can make the figure of the doctor one that is simultaneously held in awe and resented.

CURRENT CHALLENGES TO MEDICINE

These traditional characteristics of medicine as it has developed from 1945 are now being reforged by a powerful mixture of political, informational and philosophical pressures into what might be termed post-modern medicine. The particular dilemmas which drive these changes are:

• the problem of medical practice variation – similar patients treated for the same diagnosis have hugely variable outcomes depending on their clinician, hospital and geographic location. This phenomenon is both unnerving and largely unexplained;

- the soaring cost of health care throughout the western world, much of which can be explained by an ageing population and technological advance;
- the creation of an internal market in health care;
- consumerism and the consequent rise in litigation;
- the information revolution.

The problem of medical practice variation

Over the last thirty years it has been shown repeatedly that the practice of medicine varies enormously. Individual patients with identical conditions are often treated in radically different ways by highly qualified professional physicians who all claim to ascribe to the same corpus of knowledge but practice in a world that places considerable importance on 'clinical freedom'. With the advent of more sophisticated information systems, such variation between practitioners has become more visible.

> autonomy, clinical freedom, is a privilege granted to physicians (and, to a lesser extent, other professionals) by the rest of the community, who tolerate the suspension of normal processes of accountability. They do so because (to the extent that they think about it at all) they accept the proposition that this freedom results, on balance, in patients receiving more appropriate care than they would under conceivable alternatives. . . .
>
> The observation of widespread and large variations in clinical practice strikes at the heart of this argument. Physicians . . . claim that they draw on an extensive base of both scientific grounded knowledge and accumulated art and skill in selecting the interventions they will recommend and undertake. If their actual performance is, in fact, all over the map, if different practitioners respond to essentially similar . . . circumstances in very different ways, it is hard to believe that each is right in his own way. The presumption that diagnosis and therapy have a scientific basis . . . cannot be reconciled with patterns of provision which appear arbitrary and capricious.
>
> (Evans, 1990: 128)

Doctors are almost certainly not alone amongst professionals in exhibiting wide variations. They do however make larger claims than most that their actions are based in an objective scientific truth.

Soaring costs and technological advance

For clinicians, especially researchers, riding the rising wave of technological advance is exhilarating. Policy makers, caught in the undertow,

71

trying to control costs, and seemingly forever only just catching up with the breakthrough before last, find the ride less enjoyable.

The problems of exercising some control over technological advance are not of course limited to medicine.[1] However, health services are both publicly funded and arouse intense public interest. Thus Governments and third party payers throughout the developed world are trying, with increasing desperation, to contain the cost of actually delivering the service to patients and to make doctors more accountable for the public money which they spend.

Creation of an internal market in health care

One attempt, amongst many in the West, to contain costs and make doctors more accountable for the money they spend, has been the introduction of a quasi-market system for Britain's public services. The essential character-istics of the internal market within the health service are:

- cash-limited budgets;
- the rise of managerialism;
- a huge increase in bureaucracy as the contract culture takes hold;
- the target for 'blame' when something goes wrong shifting from the realm of the politician to the realm of the manager and clinician;
- diminished overall planning of services.

The creation of the internal market in health care has had at least five distinct effects on medicine. First, the status of doctors within the health care system has been downgraded. In the 1950s and 1960s doctors exerted a high degree of influence both on what services patients received and on the macro policy which determined how the NHS developed (see Figure 5.1). Managers were usually simple administrators of the system, adjudic-ating the annual contest as to which specialists should get the lion's share of this year's marginal increase in funds, but never seeking to *control* doctors whose clinical freedom to do as they wished was unchallenged.

The last ten years have changed all this (see Figure 5.2). The internal market has made clinicians responsible for limiting resource use whilst consumerism has increased patients' power. At the same time politicians have become more explicit in determining what doctors should do. This ranges from setting priorities and outcomes for the system as a whole (for example 'Health of the Nation') down to legislating quite specifically about what doctors should do in certain clinical situations.[2] Finally the administrators of the old system have been transformed into managers who see a large part of their job as controlling the professionals who work in their organisations.

Second, the stress on performance management of doctors has increased the contractual elements in medical work. This has usually occurred at the

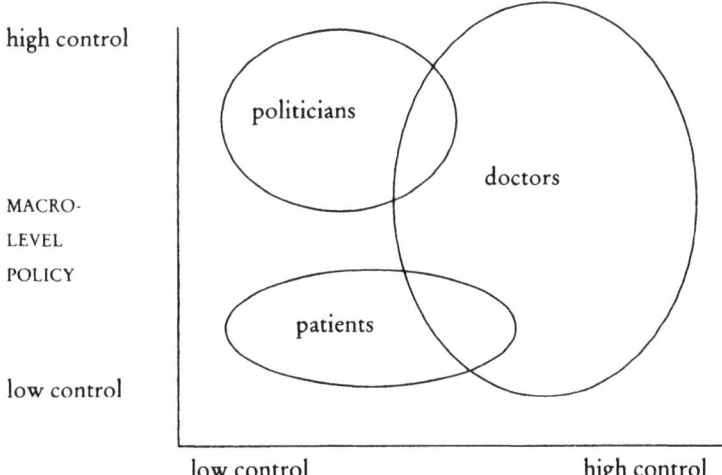

MICRO-LEVEL SERVICE: 1950s, 1960s

Figure 5.1

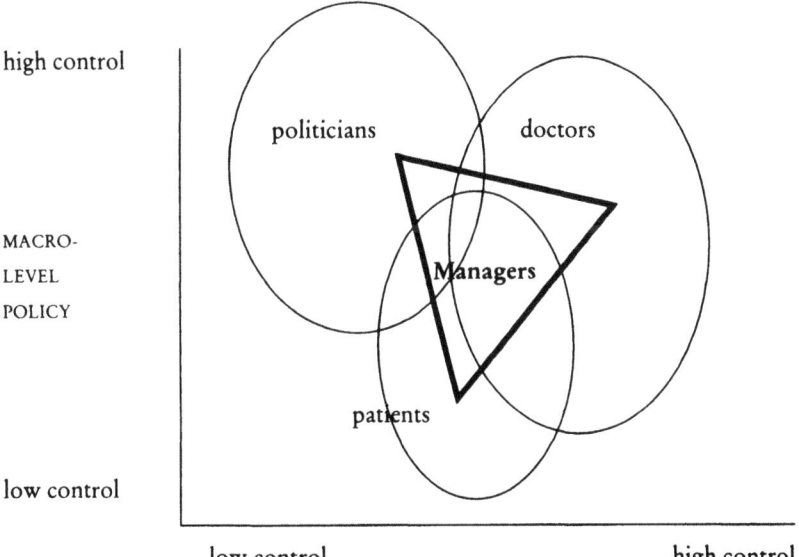

MICRO-LEVEL SERVICE: 1990s

Figure 5.2

Table 5.1 Differences in Contractual vs Professional Requirements

Requirements	Contractual	Professional
Control by:	State/funding body	Professional body/ conscience
Motivation	Compulsion	Personal responsibility
Accountability	Accountable to employer	Accountable to professional body
Priorities	Tasks given by employer	Personal judgement
Risks	Demotivation and rigidity	Professional self-interest
Flexible response to need	Diminished	Enhanced
Minimal standards	Assured	Assumed
Highest standards	Minimised	Maximised

expense of the professional self-motivation (Royal College of General Practitioners, 1996). The differences can be illustrated (Table 5.1).

Third, doctors (amongst others) are now seen to be more responsible for the system's failures than they were. As Klein says:

Perhaps the most outstanding achievement of the NHS at the end of the 1980s – just before the reforms were introduced – was that it had established itself as Britain's only immaculate institution. If there were flaws these were attributable to Government interference. If there were complaints about falling standards and mounting in-adequacies, the blame fell on ministerial niggardliness. If there was rising criticism, it fell on the heads of politicians, not providers. It is this which explains an apparent paradox. For the rest of the world, Britain's NHS offered a model of how to contain costs while still offering a universal, equitable, and reasonably adequate health service: why then, change it? For the Thatcher administration the problem posed by the NHS was that, as the 1980s progressed, there was an ever widening conflict between two policy aims: to minimise public expenditure . . . and to maximise its own political credit.

(Klein, 1995: 308)

By the mid-1990s the success of this policy, at least from the perspective of the Government, is clear. Each public failing of the NHS places not politicians, but doctors, managers, and, of course, patients in the firing line. The conflicting agendas between professional groups, questions over professional standards and issues over rationing have along the way been laid bare to public view.

Fourth, the internal market does away with 'planning', which demands a high degree of certainty and has been replaced by more flexible 'strategic' thinking. In a world of omnipresent rapid change and clinical freedom, it became harder and harder for managers and therefore the government to pin down which doctor was doing what and why. Negotiating and setting contracts constitute an attempt to regularly review the direction of service provision in such a way that physicians and managers share any risk taking. This process initially helped to make many underlying issues explicit and stimulated wider discussion and scrutiny. However, the apparent solidity of contracts, based on rational and scientific assumptions, masks the profound uncertainty that still underpins most areas of medicine at the same time as curbing the rights of doctors to exercise their own judgement. When combined with cost containment, contracts have often *increased* the pressure to take clinical risks (for example, to meet throughput targets, (Adams, 1995)) or to present a world of certainty that simply doesn't exist. It also heightens the likelihood of 'pass the parcel' when headline-hitting tragedies occur. Was it the doctor's fault or the manager's? Was it the Trust's fault or the Health Commission's? Thus far, contracts have done little to establish any meaningful method of accountability.

Finally, the Government's desire to get value for money has combined with the other pressures and forced doctors to consider the needs of the whole population and not just the patient in front of them. Whilst understandable this creates a serious dilemma: the demands of distributive justice collide with the professional duty to do the best possible for the individual patient.

Consumerism, litigation and accountability

The NHS has given birth to a generation of consumers rather than patients, who see health care as a right and are dislocated from any notion of how much it actually costs. There are no disincentives for consulting with your GP or attending a hospital casualty department other than the premium a person may or may not put on their own personal time. In the interests of reducing professional hegemony and redressing the balance of power away from the professional, patients have been encouraged by government policy (the Patients Charter) to make demands for which they pay nothing directly. This is compounded by the simultaneous explosion of post-war consumerism in every aspect of daily life and the hopes and expectations generated by media glamour giving a flavour of normality to high-tech, life-saving events. This 'rights' culture has in turn promoted and endorsed the use of litigation when rights have not been met.

Doctors have been in a weak position to defend themselves against this erosion of their power. Professional practice involves them spending huge amounts of public money and unlike any other public servant they have barely had to account for their decisions. We have relied heavily on their personal judgement.

Since the 1970s, various attempt have been made to make doctors more accountable. First, the professional organisations themselves explored ways to increase doctor accountability to their peers. Whilst this preserved core medical values it failed to account for doctor use of public resources or give patients a greater say in their treatment. Second, on the basis of somewhat crude information systems, the government reforms of 1989 endeavoured to introduce financial accountability. This initiative is commonly viewed by doctors as the dead hand of bureaucracy, inhibiting experimentation and innovation but most of all emphasising less important aspects of medicine and marginalising skills. Finally, the 1990s have seen a tentative exploration of accountability to patients. This is still in its infancy, but the rise of litigation for malpractice may well motivate doctors in Britain, as it has in the United States, to forge closer links with patients to legitimate their practice.

Doctors now find themselves potentially accountable in all three directions (the government, the professional organisations and the patients) simultaneously. To make matters even more complex accountability is currently viewed, by professionals themselves, as a means to separate the competent from the incompetent, i.e. a judgement of good and bad. Each of these interest groups has different and sometimes conflicting criteria – what is good from the point of view of one may be bad from the point of view of another. These conflicts are most clearly seen when the duty to individual patients conflicts with the desire of the professional to maximise income, or to stick to a publicly funded clinical budget.

For the medical profession not to become the battleground of these different interests, they will have to adopt a more fluid approach. Accountability can no longer be viewed as a judgement of good and bad, a means to weed out the incompetent. Instead it has to become a dynamic discussion of differences, whereby everyone is on an upward learning curve.

The information revolution

Since 1989 general practitioners, for example, have discovered that the amount which is known about their clinical practice has rapidly increased. As a direct result of the information required to make the internal market work, Health Commissions now know for the first time, practice specific admissions and death rates for major diseases, referral rates, the prescribing rates of all drugs issued by the practice and a host of demographic details derived from Census data.

Interpreting such data is as complex as devising meaningful league tables for schools or hospitals. So far managers seem to be resisting the superficial attractions such data hold for identifying poor performers. Soon however performance indicators are likely to be available (Majeed and Voss, 1995) which will purport to discriminate between 'good' and 'bad' practices. Whether such indicators actually help to improve professional standards or simply encourage regression to the mean will depend crucially on who has devised them and how they are used.

RESPONSES

The profession's response to all this change has included defensiveness, political campaigns by the BMA, acceptance by an increasing number of doctors that 'management' was inevitable and that they had as well be in there with the best. Some of these strategies succeeded better than others but, on the surface at least, the medical profession has granted the new system an acceptance which varies from the enthusiastic to the grudging.

However, all these calculated and tactical responses have occurred at other times during this century when politicians dared to meddle in medicine and in this sense there is little new in them. Underlying them however are deeper changes to medical professionalism which have been triggered or reinforced by all the factors mentioned so far. These can be summarised as:

- the movement towards Evidence-Based Medicine (EBM);
- changes in the nature and meaning of clinical freedom;
- the effect of hidden financial pressures exerted by third parties on doctors.

Evidence Based Medicine

Medicine's right to intervene in the lives of patients in intimate and potentially threatening ways, rests on its claim to superior knowledge. Over the last fifty years this knowledge base has grown exponentially and with this growth has come real improvements in health care. As discussed above variation in medical practice between doctors faced with apparently similar clinical problems poses a major threat to this claim. Why should patients or third parties endure or pay for treatments which on all the evidence are ineffective or worse?

The role and form of professional education has changed little for most practising doctors. Traditional lectures and journals continue to be their mainstay. Whilst laudable, these methods are increasingly inadequate in the face of the avalanche of new information. With the best will in the world, doctors cannot hope to keep abreast of all the latest research. The professional who has lost touch with up-to-date knowledge ceases to be the attractive proposition that so many of us rely upon.

It has taken some thirty years for this issue to reach boiling point (for a discussion of this issue see Evans, 1990) but it has finally happened. Elites within the professions in allegiance with third party payers keen to get value for money are now leading a movement to ensure that where there is good scientific evidence for a particular course of action it is acted upon. The mechanisms employed to achieve this end include:

- centralised data bases of evidence (for example, the Cochrane collaboration);[3]
- summaries of the evidence digested for busy clinicians (for example, Effective Care Bulletins);
- efforts to ensure that purchasers bring pressure to bear via contracts that are set;
- increasing numbers of protocols and guidelines which define what should be done in given circumstances;
- feedback about the number and type of treatments a doctor gives compared with those of other clinicians and audit;
- self audit and educational initiatives;
- increasing the use of marketing techniques where evidence-based medicine is 'sold' as a means to solve clinicians' problems;
- multi-faceted initiatives using many of the above.

The end of clinical freedom?

However, the nature of the professional task will change substantially if EBM becomes the accepted aim of practice. As the quality of the evidence increases then the need for doctors to exercise discretion or initiative on behalf of patients declines. Increasingly, all patients with similar conditions should be treated the same. According to this model professionalism becomes a 'God of the Gaps' existing only in the interstices of our ignorance. With the accumulation of sound knowledge, the area of medicine requiring the exercise of professional judgement will decline. But what of patients' freedom? Does good evidence limit this too? Are patients entitled to choose 'ineffective' treatments? (see Figure 5.3).

That these dilemmas are real can be seen from the case of Child B where the parents of a child with leukaemia went to court in order to try and force the local health authority to pay for an expensive and unproven third line treatment. More mundanely, what should fund holders and ENT surgeons do when they find themselves under pressure from patients to insert grommets into the ears of deaf children. This procedure, widespread till a few years ago, is now known to be largely ineffective. Yet the public have been educated to believe otherwise.

Financial incentives for doctors

The EBM movement bases its claim on the scientific evidence. As such it is often the case that the treatments it advocates are more expensive rather

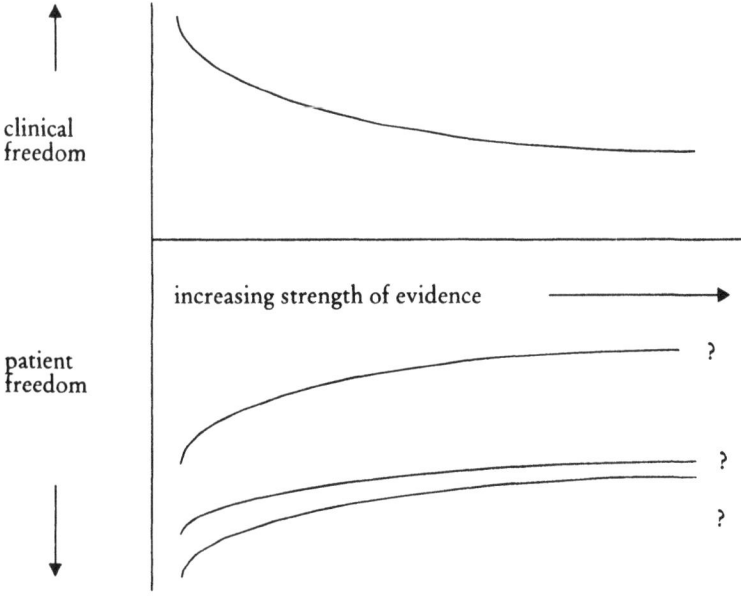

clinical
freedom

increasing strength of evidence

patient
freedom

Figure 5.3

than less. Governments and third party payers however are at least as interested in containing the costs of health care as in increasing the effectiveness of that care. To this end doctors throughout the developed world have become subject to increasingly sophisticated financial pressures from third party payers.

It has long been known that the way that doctors get paid has profound effects on the way they practice medicine: remuneration systems based on items of service tend to produce high use of resources, high physician incomes and over-servicing whilst salaried services tend to produce relatively cheaper, low-intensity health care which is bureaucratically orientated and not concerned to satisfy customers.

Over the last eight years the financial pressures on doctors in both the UK and the USA have become much more sophisticated. In Britain, fund holding GPs have taken on the responsibility for distributing public funds across their registered patients. Although initially limited to about 30 per cent of all health costs, there are now fifty pilot sites across the country who have assumed responsibility for purchasing *all* health care for their patients. Although GPs' income is not directly linked to the performance of the fund, there is clearly a potential conflict of interest between a patient wishing to get the best treatment and a GP wishing to limit cost.[4] In a similar vein, hospital consultants are under increasing pressure to meet corporate rather than clinical priorities. Such pressure is not simply about keeping within budget. It also includes subtle incentives to treat the patients of fund holders differently to those of non-fund holders; measures to ensure a minimum of bad publicity for the provider organisation; and, with league tables showing hospital mortality rates, increasing pressure to avoid high risk patients (see figure 5.4).

In the USA the movement towards for-profit providers where the provider physicians are at financial risk if their registered patients use more than the corporate average amount of resources makes these pressures intense:

> risk selection by [US healthcare providers] will become a zero-sum game, presaging fierce competition amongst doctors to avoid sick patients. Already the chief of a university hospital has admonished faculty: '[We can] no longer tolerate patients with complex and expensive-to-treat conditions being encouraged to transfer to our group.' Doctors who attract sick patients . . . risk being ostracised. . . . The gulf between clinical excellence and professional success will widen.
>
> (Woolhandler and Himmelstein, 1995: 1707.)

In many Health Maintenance Organisations (HMOs) in the States for example, physicians' salaries barely cover the costs of running their offices and employing staff. A worthwhile income can only be made if the doctor

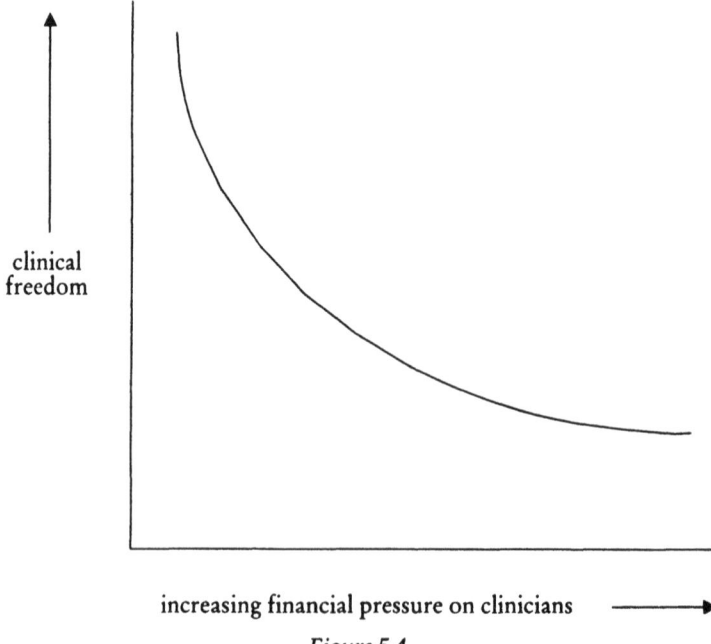

Figure 5.4

hits targets and bonuses designed to reduce resource consumption and this regime has indeed been shown to substantially reduce costs and increase profits. Woolhandler and Himmelstein (1995) in an editorial in the most respected medical journal in the USA describe the extreme pressures on US physicians in this respect and indeed one of the authors was sacked with no reason being given just prior to the publication of the editorial.

Whilst far more advanced in the USA than in Britain, in both countries physicians are under increasing pressure to keep expenditure to a minimum and in both systems this pressure is often not apparent to the patient. As this pressure for cost containment grows, so the conflict of interests becomes more pronounced: the demands of distributive justice (use this public money to the best advantage of all), and the physician's desire to maximise income conflict with the duty to do the best for each individual patient. In these circumstances it is clear that the traditional definition of professionalism (the exercise of discretion on behalf of another) no longer captures what clinicians actually do.

CULTURAL CHANGES

Any view of professionalism also has to try and take account of the meta-level changes that are occurring. In addition to those outlined already there are two further trends which are likely to affect professionals:

• from risk sharing to risk discrimination;
• the trend for organisations to change from hierarchies to webs.

First, let us consider the transfer from risk sharing to risk discrimination. The NHS has been built around sharing the economic risks of ill health. If *you* get multiple sclerosis *I* share in the costs. Whilst never made very explicit, this sharing of risks has formed a very powerful social bond. Patients frequently still say 'I know there's worse off than me – I don't want to jump the queue'. This core of social sharing has been, and is still, far more important than the associated paternalism which, perhaps inevitably, has accompanied it and it is this core which has made the British public fundamentally feel very good about their health service.

The internal market however is changing the NHS: it is increasingly important to attach the costs of individual episodes of illness to particular patients in order to bill the purchaser for the relevant amount. Such information inevitably leads to pressures to discriminate against those at high risk. After all why should purchasers or providers take on patients who are likely to use up a disproportionate share of resources if they can achieve more 'output' by operating on numerous healthy people requiring simple operations rather than risk incurring higher costs on fewer more seriously ill patients?

81

The human genome project will intensify this dilemma. Understanding the genetic component of disease means that it becomes possible to discount not just present illness but also some of the risks of future ill health. Providers of health care (along with employers) will have an incentive to define these risks since by so doing they will be able to avoid people with a potentially high risk of serious illness.

Second, let us consider the impact of moving from hierarchies to webs. The NHS is the world's biggest employer. Like most large organisations the NHS has traditionally been hierarchical with little exchange of information between its different branches. The internal market however has required much more information to be exchanged between hospitals, GPs and Health Authorities than ever before. Taken with widespread computerisation of both primary and secondary care, this has meant that much more information is available to organisations than before. This move to increasing interconnectedness reflects a similar, widespread trend in western culture. Organisations, including the NHS, are becoming:

- flatter: less hierarchical, with less emphasis on following orders from above, more on working out the appropriate local response;
- webbed: multiple small units with many horizontal as well as vertical relationships, rather than a single monolithic whole;
- higher in bandwidth: bandwidth is a metaphor for how much information is exchanged between and within organisations. The amount of information about the activity of any given unit in the NHS is now one to two orders of magnitude greater than it was ten years ago.

In general terms we are collectively moving from hierarchies to webs (Kelly, 1995). The differences are summarised in Table 5.2:

Table 5.2 The differences between hierarchies and webs.

Hierarchies	Webs
power centralised	power dispersed
control high	control low
low information flows	high information flows
slow changing	rapid response to change
little redundancy	high redundancy
prone to collapse	resilient
slow learning organisations	rapidly learning organisations
single/few goals	multiple goals
errors stigmatised	error = learning opportunity

The NHS is experiencing a mixture of these changes. Although the culture is becoming progressively web-like, the centre still exerts a high degree of control. As the internal market progresses, the inadequacy of central control becomes more apparent. This manifests itself as growing instability which will no doubt force another round of attempted central-isation. Whether this is strong enough to maintain control of the increasing centrifugal forces called forth by the market and IT remains to be seen.

Either way the move to webs is stressful for professionals who rapidly have to learn how to follow multiple goals simultaneously (balancing budgets, managing others, providing clinical care) at a time when tradi-tional certainties (my job will exist forever; my main purpose is to serve patients; doctors are superior to almost everyone) are evaporating forever.

SOME WAYS FORWARD

So far we have tried to detail some of the trends, and pressures which characterise the medical profession in the late 1990s. To summarise, these include:

- continuing high rates of technological change;
- increasing attempts by third party payers to contain costs; including the Financial Management Initiative and internal markets;
- demographic ageing of the population;
- moves to Evidence-Based Medicine;
- increasingly sophisticated consumers;
- increasing litigation;
- the information revolution with its effects on:
  patient knowledge;
  professionals' ability to place their own performance in relation to their peers;
  the move from hierarchical organisations to webs.

The pace of change is accelerating in technologies, patient attitudes and the economic status of populations. The fundamental issue facing all doctors, if they are to remain worthy of the considerable trust everyone still invests in them, is how to survive and adapt to the rapidly changing world.

Ultimately, doctors need the skills to respond quickly and appropriately to problems on the ground. An appropriate response – one that will satisfy both themselves and the various constituencies to whom they are account-able – can only be made if their isolation is reduced and they develop an understanding of the broader context.

They need to place themselves within the range of practice variation and to know how their actions may impact on other sectors of the health service. Dialogue between doctors and each of the groups to whom they are accountable can be used as an opportunity to review and develop clinical practice. This potentially enables them to hold the balance of power between the groups – thereby restoring a measure of professional autonomy – but within a more open climate, replacing the traditional professional mystique.

Finally, there is increasing acceptance within the profession that adequate clinical knowledge is not enough. To act effectively in the best interests of patients, doctors have to widen their horizons and lessen the tendency to self-reference. They need a thorough working knowledge of the system they are working within and to expand their range of skills so that, in addition to clinical competence, they are:

- financially competent;
- able to work within teams – demanding greater inter-personal skills and a broader and deeper understanding of other professionals' roles;
- proficient in the art of management, delegation, negotiation and liaison with other agencies.

All of these are helpful and, as we have discussed, have changed professionals' ideas about what it means to do their work. However, even taken together they fail to deal with many of the challenges which professionals face.

At the start of this chapter we defined a professional task as

one which requires the immediate exercise of discretion or initiative on behalf of another in a situation of complexity.

In an increasingly complex world it is quite clear that some people will continue to exercise discretion or initiative on behalf of others. We believe that in order to do this well the definition of a professional task should be amended to one where:

one person exercises discretion or initiative *with* another in a situation of complexity *ensuring so far as possible that all necessary information, together with any financial incentives and constraints which the professional may be under, are transparent to the patient or client.*

This major extension of the professional task will not be achieved easily. In particular it is likely to depend on sophisticated information technology. However, such extension does not spell the end of professionalism – rather its successful adaptation to a rapidly changing world.

NOTES

1 See Winner (1986) for a discussion of the social and professional effects of rapid technological advances.
2 The 1990 GP contract laid legal obligations on doctors to provide particular services for groups of patients to promote health. There is some doubt as to whether this move to allow politicians to dictate clinical practice is effective.
3 The Cochrane Collaboration is an international project to collate all the evidence relating to particular medical topics. The quality of the evidence is

then assessed and where possible summary recommendations are made. In the UK the results are made available to clinicians via short Effective Care Bulletins.

4 Interestingly the evidence so far seems to indicate that fund holders have sometimes improved hotel aspects of care but shows very little difference so far as referral rates, or prescribing costs are concerned when compared to non-fundholding colleagues.

REFERENCES

Adams, C. (1995) 'The OXDONS Syndrome: The inevitable disease of the NHS reforms', *British Medical Journal*, 311: 1559–61.

Evans, R. (1990) 'The dog in the night: Medical practice variations and health policy', in T. Anderson and G. Mooney (eds) *The Challenges of Medical Practice Variations*, London: Macmillan, 117–52.

Kelly, K. (1995) *Out of Control: The New Biology of Machines*, New York: Random House.

Klein, R. (1995) 'Big Bang health reform – does it work? The case of Britain's 1991 health reforms', *Millbank Quarterly*, 73: 299–337.

Majeed, F. and Voss, S. (1995) 'Performance indicators for General Practice', *British Medical Journal*, 311: 209–10.

Raine, J.W. and Willson, M.J. (1993) *Managing Criminal Justice*, New York, London: Harvester Wheatsheaf.

Royal College of General Practitioners (1996) 'The nature of General Medicare Practice. Report for General Practice 27'.

Winner, L. (1986) *The Whale And The Reactor*, Chicago: Chicago University Press.

Woolhandler, S. and Himmelstein, D. (1995) Editorial, *New England Journal of Medicine*, 333:1707.

6

REGENERATING PROFESSIONALISM WITHIN THE ACADEMIC WORKPLACE

Jon Nixon

INTRODUCTION

Professionalism is a claim which particular occupational groups make about the values implicit in the institutional practices for which they are responsible. Traditionally, those values have involved a strong service orientation. However, the policy of creating quasi markets within which services compete for limited resources, together with a steadily rising level of expectation and demand among particular client groups, has occasioned a crisis within many of the more established professions. At the same time it has prompted the emergence of new professional groups, and new professionally defined tasks, within traditionally non-professional occupational structures. Professional values, in other words, can no longer be uncomplicatedly equated with a public service value orientation. What we are witnessing, as Freidson (1994) has argued, is 'professionalism reborn'.

It is from this perspective that the present chapter seeks to explore the changing role of what within the American tradition is termed 'faculty'. (Significantly, no such collective noun exists in the British system. Those terms that do exist tend to relate either to task and function, as in the case of 'lecturing staff' or 'university teachers', or to status, as in the case of 'non professorial staff' as opposed to the 'professoriat'.) The conditions of higher education, it is argued, have occasioned a crisis of professional identity precisely because there is no agreement – indeed, no serious public debate – regarding the values and purposes of higher education. We have to go back over thirty years to locate a 'moment' when higher education as a topic focused and infused the wider public and academic debate on the moral purposes and social ends of education.

DEFINING MOMENT OR LOST OPPORTUNITY?

On 7 May 1959, C. P. Snow (then Sir Charles, soon to be Lord Snow) delivered the annual Rede lecture on the subject of 'The Two Cultures and the Scientific Revolution'.[1] On the face of it this was a fairly unremarkable

86

event involving a fairly unremarkable public figure. However, in retro-spect, it can be viewed as a significant moment in what passes for the continuing public debate on the role of higher education in post-war Britain. In spite of Snow's highly selective and at times hostile character-isation of the values represented by the literary culture, his lecture succeeded in highlighting a number of emergent themes that still deter-mine the parameters of policy making as it relates to higher education:

- the increasing importance of technical fields of study, of applied scientific modes of enquiry and, more recently, of inventive work within the new technologies;
- the need for a more highly trained workforce with the flexibility to respond promptly to the changing demands of the market and to technological advances across a variety of fields;
- the changing purposes of higher education given the new demands placed upon it (including the demand for greater 'social usefulness').

Snow had nicely caught the modernising mood of the time: Harold Wilson, in his famous 1964 election speech, was about to produce his 'big idea' – 'the white heat of the technological revolution' – and give it a sharp, educational twist through his support for a University of the Air (later the Open University); Concorde – that controversial symbol of technological aspiration – was about to find its zealous champion in the person of Tony Benn, who headed the newly established Ministry of Technology (with Snow second-in-command and acting as government spokesman on technology in the House of Lords between 1964 and 1966); and higher education, as the Robbins Committee (1963) partially foresaw, was about to embark on an extended period of student expansion and institutional proliferation. Who could possibly doubt that it was the scientists and technocrats who, in Snow's phrase, 'had the future in their bones'?

There was much public support for Snow and very little dissent from what, to one acute and acerbic observer, was becoming a new orthodoxy: the assumption of increased prosperity through technological and scien-tific progress. F. R. Leavis waited three years to respond to Snow and took as his opportunity an invitation to deliver the 1962 Richmond lecture at Downing College, Cambridge, in the year of his retirement.[2] The tone Leavis adopted in this lecture was utterly uncompromising. Indeed, even to a fellow member of the literary culture who partially supported the substance of Leavis's critique, its tone was 'impermissible' (Trilling, 1966: 150). Leavis inveighed against what he saw as Snow's careless misreading of particular writers, and traditions of critical and humanistic scholarship, whose social usefulness could not be measured in terms of technological progress. Much more was at issue, however, than the reputation of particular writers within the literary canon. The underlying issue was Snow's evident enthusiasm for those modernising tendencies which, to

Leavis, would lead inevitably to a calamitous reduction of human experience and the consequent loss of moral agency. The prime role of the university, argued Leavis, was to acknowledge moral complexity by engaging with what he termed 'the third realm': the realm of 'perception, knowledge, judgement and responsibility' (1972: 63). It is this 'third realm' – 'neither merely private and personal nor public in the sense that it can be brought into the laboratory and pointed to' (p. 62) – which according to Leavis provides the university with whatever social usefulness it might have.

In many respects history has supported Snow's view of the way the world is changing, though not necessarily the moral construction Snow placed upon change. Leavis was right to insist that the changes identified by Snow raise inescapable issues of value that require moral choices. He was also right to point up the extent to which, and ways in which, Snow's argument deployed the notion of 'progress' in order to foreclose on any serious and sustained exploration of the moral dimensions of change. With hindsight, what we see in the policy developments of the last thirty years is not so much 'progress' as a continuing failure to address the moral dilemmas thrown up by the changing conditions of higher education.

THE CHANGING CONDITIONS OF HIGHER EDUCATION

The challenge facing higher education, then, must in part be understood *historically* in terms of (a) the dramatic expansion in student numbers over the last thirty years together with a steady reduction in the unit of resource, (b) the consequent changes in curriculum, teaching and assessment, and (c) changes in the conditions of academic work. But it must also be understood *morally* in terms of the ways in which these changes impact upon the lives of particular individuals and groups and on the quality of learning. Higher education is undergoing a series of complex, overlapping changes, which are profoundly affecting its organisational structures, its traditional practices and – crucially – the way in which its institutions, and those who work within them, are viewed by the public.

The changing student body

From 1963 to 1990 expansion far exceeded the expectations of the Robbins Committee (1963) which had looked forward to a continuing modest expansion of higher education within a system not fundamentally different from the previous one of highly restricted access: in 1962 the total number of full-time students in the higher education system was 216,000; by 1989–90, including home and overseas students, part-timers in universities, the Open University, the then polytechnics and other colleges offering advanced courses, it was 1,086,300 (Halsey, 1992a). Expansion has brought with it a much less homogeneous student population. While children of working-class families and members of some minority ethnic groups continue to be under-represented, women and part-time students now make up a greater proportion of the total (with the growth in participation by women being a particular feature of the new universities and of part-time courses). The age profile is also changing: 'Between 1981 and 1991 the number of mature first year students on undergraduate courses almost tripled, from 26,000 to over 70,000, such that nearly one in three entrants were aged 21 and over by the end of this period' (Parry, 1995: 110). Overall the pattern of student entry was such that, by 1990, more mature students entered higher education in Great Britain than young students, with 80 per cent of all mature students located in the new universities (NCE, 1993: 293). The traditional image of transition at 18-plus from school or college to university is, for the majority of institutions, becoming an anachronism.

Changes in curriculum, teaching and assessment

These changes in the student population have led to diversification of course content and structure and to an increased emphasis on differentiating the educational needs of students, with modularisation and credit accumulation and transfer now established as important organisational elements in the old as well as the new universities. The shift is away 'from an early notion of access based on defined routes and discrete courses to one more centrally concerned with the "accessibility" of institutions and the suitability and flexibility of their curricula for a diverse student audience' (Parry, 1995: 125). Entwistle (1992) has summarised some of the main elements of that shift in terms of the kinds of teaching methods currently being practised within the context of higher education: lectures; resource-based learning, open learning and distance education; instructional technology and computer-based learning; discussion classes and simulations; peer teaching and co-operative project work; and supervised work experience and learning contracts. What is important about these current practices, argues Entwistle, is not just the variety of methods adopted, but the emphasis placed upon 'self-regulated learning' and upon students becoming increasingly aware of their own studying and thinking processes; an emphasis which is also evident in the shift towards 'formative' assessment procedures including self- and peer assessment and the development of 'learner agreements' (Opacic, 1994).

Changing conditions of academic work

Alongside the changing patterns of student intake and of curriculum and pedagogy are immense changes in the staffing structures of higher education. A recent OECD study of institutional management in higher education argues that the cohesion afforded by traditional structures 'is likely to be eroded as status and other differentials increase, especially between staff with permanent appointments and those in temporary or part-time contracts'. The report goes on to argue that 'it is no longer sensible to speak of a single academic profession' and that 'a caste distinction is emerging between "have" and "have-not" groups'. The latter constitute 'an underclass . . . with limited prospects for advancement or employment stability'. At the same time increased differentials and tensions are apparent among what the report calls 'top-level academics' who are under pressure to produce high-profile research and to develop and market new and appealing courses (Kogan, Moses and El-Khawas, 1994: 62–3). The result is that different and often incompatible structures are emerging with different groups occupied on different tasks and often pursuing different interests. Meanwhile, much of the day-to-day work of teaching and research in universities is sustained by 'a growing army of insecurely employed contract staff who now make up to a third of all academic employees' (Ainley, 1994: 32).

A CRISIS OF PROFESSIONAL IDENTITY

A consequence of the changing conditions outlined above is that the occupation of university teacher no longer automatically carries the assumption of autonomy and status. Since autonomy and status have been defining characteristics of occupations that lay claim to being professions, these changes have occasioned some debate as to what kind of occu- pational group, or groups, university teachers now constitute, and have consequently increased many of the tensions inherent in the role of the university teacher.

The key questions in the debate concern the extent to which university teachers now constitute (a) a profession divided against itself, (b) a set of occupations so diverse in their practices that the term 'professional' may no longer be applicable in all or even most cases, or (c) a new proletariat with very little opportunity, and even less encouragement, to exercise independent judgement and self-regulation.

A divided profession?

The role of university teacher, as Piper (1994) has argued, is Janus-faced: 'academics look to their occupation for their identity as teachers, but outside for their identity as subject specialists' (p. 6). This dual professional identity is becoming increasingly difficult to sustain, both at the level of professional practice and at the level of organisational structure. The changing student intake has placed an emphasis on the need for pedagogical and curriculum change and, consequently, on the professional identity of the university teacher *as teacher*, capable of developing and marketing innovative programmes. At the same time, however, the changing conditions of academic work have placed a premium on the professional identity of the university teacher *as researcher*, capable of attracting external funds within an increasingly competitive research culture.

The system requires of university lecturers an increased investment not only in their own institutions, but in the professional and business communities and the various networks and structures that comprise their particular fields and subject specialisms. Career mobility, moreover, depends increasingly on the individual's reputation and influence outside their own institution: 'Spending time with colleagues does not generate research grants and seldom results in publications. Nor does it advance disciplinary knowledge. The incentives to generate and participate in an intellectual life on a university campus are small in comparison to the incentives to engage in an intellectual life off campus' (Steneck, 1994: 19). Increasingly, the pull is outward and upward.

A plurality of occupations?

This situation has led to a greater degree of institutional specialisation and to sharper divisions of labour within the academic workplace. As a result of this increased stratification, the professional identity of university teachers is being redefined: 'Through diversification, several categories of academic workers have been created, each having distinct terms and conditions of employment, including salary scales, benefits, career chances, duties and prerogatives in university governance' (Newson and Buchbinder, 1988: 25). Within the UK these categories, and the differentials between them, are being reinforced through the introduction of teaching-only contracts, the development of specialist research centres and graduate schools within existing institutions, differentiated pay scales, independently negotiated pay settlements for senior academics and an increasing reliance on research-contract staff. The academic workforce, in other words, now includes a plurality of occupational groups divided from one another by task, influence and seniority within the institution.

The recent emphasis within curriculum design on modular programmes of work and associated systems of assessment has reinforced these divisions through the creation of a 'middle management' tier of course leaders or what Winter (1995) calls 'academic managers': 'Responsibility for the overall coherence and progression of students' education is assumed not by the staff who teach individual modules but by the academic managers who design the modular system and by the academic counsellors who guide student choice of modules' (p. 134). This diversification of the academic workforce is accompanied, both within the UK and elsewhere, by stratification of the student body: 'research-focused graduate students and full-time professors are in a preferred status while teaching-oriented part-timers and classroom-oriented graduates are in a secondary status' (Buchbinder and Rajagopal, 1995: 70).

A new proletariat?

Halsey (1992b) argues that the fragmentation of the academic workplace is one of a number of material and ideological conditions which, taken together, are transforming university teachers into a new proletariat whose relative class and status advantages are being significantly eroded:

Managerialism gradually comes to dominate collegiate cooperation in the organisation of both teaching and research. Explicit vocationalism displaces implicit vocational preparation, as degree courses are adapted to the changing division of labour in the graduate market. Research endeavours are increasingly applied to the requirements of government or industrial demands. The don becomes increasingly a salaried or even a piece-work labourer in the service of an expanding middle class of administrators and technologists.

(Halsey, 1992b: 13)

While no-one would disagree that university teachers are in a very different position to, say, craft workers in the nineteenth-century textile industry, Halsey and others would argue that both groups share a lack of 'ideological' control over their work: 'Through their command of discrete expertise, academics can still largely influence the processes of both their research and teaching, but the raw material (students or problems to be investigated) is increasingly determined by the combined influences of the state, institutional managers and the market' (Miller, 1995: 56). These combined influences help create a climate that, according to Dummett (1994), is underpinned by the 'principles' of insecurity, competition and surveillance:

that each task must be done at the least possible cost; that people work effectively only if they know their jobs are insecure, and if they are lured by increases of salary or of status to be obtained in competition with their colleagues; and that no institution can be trusted to evaluate its own or its employees' efficiency, which must be estimated by having each employee assessed by other employees or by the 'customers' by 'objective' performance indicators or, best of all, by the reports of external inspectors.

(p. 1269)

A PROFESSIONAL PERSPECTIVE ON LEARNING

Scott (1995: 9–10) has recently argued that the transition from elite to mass higher education cannot be understood simply in terms either of the evolution of higher education systems, such as the expansion of student numbers or structural reforms; or of the substitution of one paradigm, labelled 'mass', for another labelled 'elite'. Instead, it must be interpreted 'in the context of the restless synergy between plural modernisations – of the academy, polity, economy, society and culture'. Central to this 'restless synergy' is the changing role of professionals and the altered ground of their claim to professionalism. The significant shift is at the level of values and underlying structures of belief; structures that are in new and vital interplay with emergent forms of professional agency.

Yet none of the characterisations of 'the professional', as outlined in the previous section, adequately acknowledges the capacity of university teachers to define their own occupational values and to construct their professional identity around those values. That failure to acknowledge professional 'voice' is itself a measure of the extent to which an earlier emphasis on professional 'autonomy' and 'status' has given way to a preoccupation with structural constraint. The university, as Kerr (1995: 26) points out, 'has become bigger and more complex, more tensed with checks and balances'. Likening the university to a city, Kerr spells out some of the implications of that complexity:

> Some get lost in the city; some rise to the top within it; most fashion their lives within one of its many subcultures. There is less sense of community than in the village but also less of confinement. There is less sense of purpose than within the town but there are more ways to excel. There are also more refuges for anonymity – both for the creative person and the drifter. As against the village and the town, the 'city' is more like the totality of civilisation as it has evolved and more an integral part of it; and movement to and from the surrounding society has been greatly accelerated.
>
> (p. 31)

It is hardly surprising that within this complex institutional setting – with its multiplicity of 'purpose', its potential for 'refuge' and 'anonymity', its permeation by 'the surrounding society' – no single 'professional voice' is to be heard. Nevertheless, university teachers bring important insights to bear on their own practice and, as this central section of the chapter tries to show, these insights constitute an important perspective on the nature of learning and the institutional conditions necessary for learning to flourish.

The analysis presented in this section is based on interviews conducted with two groups of university teachers in two different institutions of higher education: an 'old' and a 'new' university. Thirty interviews were conducted overall, fifteen within each institution (with an equal number of female and male interviewees overall). Interviews lasted about an hour and took the form of a structured discussion around an agreed set of issues. The particular fields within which interviewees were working were as follows: Animal and Plant Sciences, Biblical Studies, Biomedical Sciences, Business Studies, Computer Science, Cultural Studies, Engineering, English Studies, Law, Management Studies, Marketing, Philosophy, Physics, Probability and Statistics, Restorative Dentistry, Sociology, and Town and Regional Planning.

A report on the initial round of interviews was discussed in a number of forums within the two institutions concerned and with staff from other institutions (Nixon, 1995a). This paper draws on that original interview data, on further data drawn from follow-up interviews in each of the institutions, and on comments and insights offered in subsequent discussions and seminars (see also Nixon, 1996). In its emphasis on practitioners' perceptions of the values underlying their own practice, the analysis complements research undertaken in school settings (Nixon, 1995b) and in the context of public inspection and support services (Nixon and Rudduck, 1994). In the argument it develops about professionalism (though not in the data it draws on) it owes much to continuing discussions conducted in the context of the ESRC-funded project, *New Forms of Education Management* (see Nixon *et al.*, 1996, forthcoming).[3]

The centrality of learning: the nature and purposes of learning

From the interview data emerges a view of learning, not as something that happens to students, but as something that they themselves must make happen. Learning is active and pressing and invariably involves change, which is why its most significant outcomes can never be pre-specified with certainty. A consequence of conceptualising learning in this way is that student motivation becomes a major pedagogical concern. If motivation is seen not as a precondition of learning but as a vital and active constituent of learning, then student motivation itself becomes central to the task of higher education.

(i) **Independent learning: promoting responsibility for learning**
Interviewees emphasised the importance of students thinking for themselves:

> I encourage students to think for themselves and try to help them acquire background knowledge that they can use in different situations. For example, a course I'm teaching at the moment is perforce very technique-oriented – certain procedures have to be carried out in a relatively short time. I could just tell the students how to carry

out each item of work as a set of rules, but I've tried to teach it in a different way by looking at the teeth we are treating and starting to discuss the problems we would encounter in trying to restore them. Then we look at the materials that are available for use in these situations, the needs and requirements of these materials and their characteristics, and the recognised techniques that might be adopted. Finally the group discusses the merits of these techniques and are able to use their knowledge for the demonstrations they are required to prepare. Hence they end up with a greater likelihood of being able to understand the concepts behind techniques and are able to adapt their knowledge to many different situations. My hope is that at the end of the day the students will be able to think for themselves.

Other interviewees offered similar accounts. One lecturer whose courses focus more specifically on a particular body of literature emphasised that he 'would want students to respect the material and to be sensitive to it, but to engage with it, rather than seeing it as a museum piece – to use it as a spur for their own reflections and writings'. Another interviewee working as a specialist within an interdisciplinary field of study spoke of how, within his teaching, 'the content is important, but it's not as important as trying to stimulate students to think for themselves and to interact with one another about the ideas and issues under discussion'.

(ii) **Learning as dialogue: encouraging co-operative learning**   'I look at the level, quality and amount of debate between students', emphasised one interviewee. Others stressed the importance of entering into that dialogue as interested participants: 'Everything that we do as academics ought to reflect our enthusiasms, interests, doubts and dilemmas regarding the things we teach.' So conceived, learning is a three-cornered conversation between the student, the teacher and the object of enquiry: 'When the teaching's going well I always feel that I'm learning as well as the students. We might be learning different things and at different levels but we are all learning.' Such a conception favours group work and interactional methods of study, but by no means rules out the extended exposition of the lecture form as a valuable means of focusing debate and furthering enquiry. What matters is that the teaching method adopted allows for a serious engagement with differing viewpoints, including those of the teacher and of any texts or materials that are presented for consideration.

(iii) **Relevant learning: enhancing capability and application**   Complex learning is not a matter of first acquiring particular facts and skills and then applying these within particular contexts, for in any intellectually demanding task there are always facts and skills that can only be acquired through application. Any course which aims to challenge and make intellectual demands on students must be concerned, therefore, with providing opportunities for them to learn through application. In the following account, for example, an interviewee explains the educational value of a recently established 'law clinic', in which law students offer free legal advice to students from across the institution:

> Students are certainly grasping legal concepts better as a result of their experience in the clinic. That's what is so valuable about it. Let me try and explain how it works. A problem comes through the door in the form of a client. You don't know what that problem is, other than that the client has made an appointment and has said something like, 'I've been injured in a road traffic accident'. Students interview clients on their own, so they're in control throughout the interview. I'm not breathing down their necks. Only after they have conducted the interview with the client do they come and talk with me. The student will say, 'These are the facts of the case as I understand them'. And I'll say something like, 'Well, what issues of law do we have here?' They'll say, 'Well, there's the accident and there must be something about compensating people who are injured as a result of road traffic accidents'. So I'll say, 'OK, but what's the cause of action? What legal principle is at stake?' In this case the student might say, 'I suppose it's tort, is it?' I'd reply, 'Yes, it is, but let's be more specific'. Eventually I get out of them that it's something called 'negligence'. They say, 'Ah, of course, it's actually a case of negligence this!', and they see that this is an instance of a general legal principle that applies to a wide variety of cases. They grasp the principle by having to apply it to the problem that walks through the door.

The assumptions upon which the 'law clinic' is based were shared and articulated by interviewees from a wide range of intellectual backgrounds and fields of study. For example, an interviewee from Computer Science argued: 'you can't abstract the skills from the contexts in which those skills are put to work – and that has tremendous implications for the way we teach and design our courses'; while another interviewee who taught on a variety of courses within the field of Probability and Statistics argued: 'I try to embed the techniques and procedures of my discipline in tasks that have relevance and require some practical engagement by the students'. The emphasis on learning through application does not, in other words, distinguish particular fields of study, but is central to the entire higher education curriculum – although, of course, it will have very different pedagogical and organisational implications for different areas of the curriculum.

(iv) Learning as partnership: working across institutional divides

The emphasis on application requires a strong commitment to partnership and to working across institutional divides. Interviewees spoke of the importance of enabling students to develop work-related skills and of developing and sustaining links with employers: 'We couldn't possibly have developed this course without close and continuing consultation with industry.' Experience of the workplace was an essential part of many of the courses on which interviewees taught and this necessitated close liaison with other professional groups: 'It's essential that they understand the rationale of the course. They're not simply providing a placement. They're working with us to reinforce the learning that has already taken place and to develop new dimensions of learning.'

(v) **Learning as a public good: developing commitment to social ends** Several of the interviewees spoke of the importance of incorporating into their teaching some discussion of values and/or professional ethics. As one interviewee pointed out, this dimension of learning has often been neglected in the past:

> We've sent people out to be general practitioners, or engineers or teachers without discussing with them what it means to be a doctor, an engineer or a teacher. Perhaps in the past that wasn't so necessary, because even in the private sector there was a consensus around the old public service values. That's no longer the case, so unless we put values on the agenda we could end up with a society of highly competent but ethically illiterate professionals. That's not a prospect that I find particularly inviting.

Other interviewees emphasised that this was not just a pedagogical issue but a question of how learning is perceived and valued both within and outside institutions of higher education: 'We really do need to see learning as a resource that's going to help everyone. That means that students have to shoulder some big responsibilities, but it also means that in educating young people the state is protecting its own future.' Another interviewee presented the issue even more sharply:

> We are so grudging in this country. It's as if society is doing students some great favour by educating them. Of course, that's because our society is based on such individualist principles – it's just assumed that students are in it purely for their own gain. But there's great altruism and self-sacrifice among very many young people that I come into contact with. If only as a society we would draw on it! It's the old problem of low, mean-minded expectations.

(v) **Learning as lifelong: establishing dispositions and habits of mind** Interviewees emphasised the rapid turnover both in knowledge and in ways of knowing and stressed the need for higher education to prepare students for life in a rapidly changing society. Some saw this in terms of inculcating certain attitudes to knowledge: 'I try to get across that knowledge is hugely important but provisional. What matters is that one is willing to go on learning and to acquire new skills and know-how.' One interviewee considered that her own discipline of scientific enquiry carried with it the dispositions and habits of mind necessary for becoming a lifelong learner: 'Science is not just a matter of acquiring scientific knowledge (whatever that is!), but of thinking scientifically and adopting the habits and dispositions of the scientist. Having studied science no student should ever come at any problem in quite the same way again.'

Collegiality as an organisational principle: the institutional conditions of learning

In considering the institutional conditions necessary for learning to flourish interviewees raised questions about collegiality, about the quality of participation, about support for professional development and about opportunities for research and for research-based teaching.

(i) **Discourse as a way of life** Interviewees spoke of the importance of collegiality and of the need for mutually supportive relationships with colleagues: 'The ideal of the "good life" has to be discovered on the corridor and in the staff room, in all our various meetings with one another. Universities are about ideas and our professional relationships must be directed at keeping ideas alive.' They highlighted the value of professional relationships across departments and of the need for inter-disciplinarity in course development, planning and evaluation. They also, however, spoke of their own sense of professional isolation and of the competitive atmosphere that prevails within and across certain de-partments. Some felt strongly that the drive towards greater efficiency, cost effectiveness and accountability had significantly raised the level of stress and put great pressure on particular categories of staff (those, for example, working in minority interest areas and those on part-time and temporary contracts). These factors, they claimed, exacerbate the problem of professional isolation, thereby making it that much more difficult to engage, as colleagues, in serious interdisciplinary debate about the quality of provision. The creation of a sense of community and a willingness to examine values openly are not, by this reckoning, some kind of optional extra. They are the necessary conditions for constructing a context within which questions relating to 'quality' can be taken seriously.

(ii) **Consultation and participation** Interviewees also spoke of the importance of having a clear sense of where their own institution was going; a sense of its priorities and long-term commitments. They stressed the need for close consultation across the various layers of institutional management and for a recognition that their own concerns and profes-sional interests counted in the strategic planning of the institution as a whole. While interviewees acknowledged the aspirations of their institu-tion towards a consultative style of management, several of them spoke of their own feelings of alienation and, as one of them put it, a sense of 'not being in the know'. Another spoke more bluntly: 'They're forever switching the goal posts. It makes you feel jumpy – on edge. You never know what you're going to have to react to next.' The result is that some staff feel unable to commit themselves to any long-term planning or to take any initiative beyond their immediate sphere of responsibility. This only serves to deepen the sense of alienation, thereby establishing a downward spiral of powerlessness. The achievement of a real sense of professional identity and continuity across all grades and categories of staff is essential.

(iii) Support for professional development   In the main interviewees felt that there were few structures in place to support their own professional development as teachers and researchers. Financial support for attending conferences varied across institutions and departments, with the emphasis on attendance at conferences for the purpose of delivering academic papers. However, as one interviewee pointed out, there is also a need for updating oneself on pedagogical and policy developments: 'I wanted to go to that conference to find out. If I'd been delivering a paper there'd have been no problem. They'd have coughed up. But I wasn't in a position to offer a paper. I needed to know about what was happening in this area. My head of department really just wasn't interested and the funding wasn't forthcoming.' Across departments support for professional development varies enormously, both in terms of the systems that are put in place and in terms of the commitment invested by the head of department and senior personnel. 'It's such a competitive culture', remarked one interviewee, 'once you've become a Reader or Professor, you're really just protecting your own interests. Seniority's not about looking after people any more. Perhaps it never was.'

(iv) Equal opportunities for research   The increasing demand for research activity has occasioned considerable anxiety among teachers in higher education and this anxiety was reflected in interviewees' comments. The research dimension of their work was, without exception, held to be of importance in its own right and, with a very few exceptions, seen as integral to the task of teaching. However, almost all those who were interviewed felt some tension between their teaching responsibilities and research commitments. Many felt that they had insufficient time to conduct research to their satisfaction and a few acknowledged that they had given up on research altogether. (The particularly heavy teaching load experienced by some interviewees within the 'new' university setting exacerbated these problems.) Others had persevered, but felt that the dominant view of what constitutes research militates against any attempt to integrate it into their current teaching practice. The problem, as one interviewee emphasised, is cultural as well as structural: 'We need to find new ways of thinking about research – new ways of acknowledging its diversity. Discussion about research is invariably restricted to just two questions: How much money will it bring in? and How many publications will it generate? There's got to be more to it than that!' The development of a research tradition within which a variety of research aims, processes and outcomes are valued and actively encouraged is of the utmost importance in ensuring that research and teaching work together in the educational interests of the student.

IMPLICATIONS FOR HIGHER EDUCATION

Higher education, I have argued, has undergone immense changes over the last thirty years. These changes, involving the fragmentation of the academic workplace together with increased differentials between individuals in respect of status and autonomy, have had a profound effect on the role of university teachers and on their professional identity. As the previous section tried to show, however, university teachers have important insights to bring to the debate on higher education; insights into the nature of learning and into the institutional conditions necessary for learning to flourish. What we may infer from these insights is the emergence of a new professionalism constructed around the notion of the university teacher as educator. Any effective restructuring of higher education must take on board the changing professional identity of university teachers and, in so doing, come to terms with the implications of that changing identity for the management of higher education.

This will involve:

1 The recognition of teaching as an important area of professional expertise in its own right – and of the need for structures of professional development and support to ensure the growth of that expertise.

   Teaching is one of the main activities of the university lecturer. However, career promotion in both old and new universities is usually based upon research activity and/or administrative responsibility. Excellence in teaching is taken for granted, rarely acknowledged and even more rarely rewarded. Institutions of higher education should recognise teaching as a core activity that requires clearly defined structures of professional support and career development. Excellence in teaching must be a defining feature of 'professionalism' within the context of higher education.

2 The reintegration of teaching and research – and the need for structures to facilitate collegiality within and across departments and between individuals with increasingly different workloads and professional commitments.

   Research activity is becoming increasingly separated from the practice of teaching. This can only have the effect of further fragmenting the academic workforce and increasing the already considerable tensions among academic staff. Griffith (1995: 45) has noted the movement towards the creation of three clearly distinguished types of university: 'those 20 or so which receive 75% of available research grants; those which are enabled to conduct research in a few specialisms; and the majority which receive little or no research money at all'. Within each of these categories the divisions of labour are also becoming sharper and less permeable. Institutions of higher education should seek to re-integrate teaching and research through collegial structures that encourage interdisciplinary dialogue at every level. The ability to relate teaching to research – to ensure that teaching is research-based – is a further defining feature of 'professionalism' within the higher education context.

3 A recognition of the wide variety of research traditions and outcomes – and the need for structures to ensure that all research activity is valued for its contribution to the overall work of the institution.

High-profile research tends to be empirical, externally funded and fixed-term. It also, increasingly, tends to address policy issues or issues that are acknowledged to be of public concern. This has led to some powerful research programmes that can be expected to impact significantly on policy and practice within specific fields. The danger is, however, that other research traditions that have helped define the notion of systematic enquiry will be lost from view. These traditions include 'critical theory', 'humanistic scholarship', much of what has come to be termed 'blue sky' research, and 'action research'. Smith and Brown (1995), for example, have argued strongly for research into the teaching and learning processes within higher education and for this to be recognised as a core research activity within all institutions of higher education. 'Professionalism' within higher education must be defined in terms of the ability to adopt and sustain a research perspective. The task facing institutions of higher education is to ensure that this perspective remains open and eclectic, while upholding the criteria of excellence pertaining within the various traditions.

This chapter has tried to show that there is a coherent 'professional' perspective on teaching and learning in higher education; a 'professionalism' that is ideologically constructed around particular sets of values and practices. In planning for the future, those with responsibility for managing higher education, and for broad policy decisions in the area of higher education, would do well to consider the implications of that perspective. To ignore it is to ensure that the restructuring of higher education will be both piecemeal and, inevitably, driven by a very different set of values. What is at stake is not only the survival of a 'profession', but the survival of those values that have helped define the structures and practices of higher education.

NOTES

1 The text of the Rede lecture was published in *Encounter* in two parts, in June and July 1959. This, together with a later piece entitled 'A Second Look', was published in 1964 by Cambridge University Press. Both pieces were reprinted in 1993 with an authoritative introduction by Stefan Collini.
2 This was printed in Leavis, 1972. In the same volume is a lecture delivered in 1966 in which Leavis returned to particular themes in the controversy.
3 The *New Forms of Education Management* project is funded by the ESRC as part of its *Local Governance Programme*. The research team comprises Stewart Ranson (Director), Jane Martin, Penny McKeown and Jon Nixon.

REFERENCES

Ainley, P. (1994) *Degrees of Difference: Higher Education in the 1990s*, London: Lawrence & Wishart.

Buchbinder, H. and Rajagopal, P. (1995) 'Canadian universities and the impact of austerity on the academic workplace', in J. Smyth (ed.) *Academic Work: The Changing Labour Process in Higher Education*, Buckingham: SRHE/Open University Press, 60–73.

Dummett, M. (1994) 'Too many cooks and a capitalist flavour', *The Tablet*, Educational Supplement No. 71 (8 October), 1268–9.

Entwistle, N. (1992) *The Impact of Teaching on Learning Outcomes in Higher Education: A Literature Review*, Sheffield: Committee of Vice-Chancellors and Principals, Universities' and Colleges' Staff Development Agency.

Freidson, E. (1994) *Professionalism Reborn: Theory, Prophesy and Policy*, Cambridge: Polity Press.

Griffith, J. (1995) *Research Assessment*, London: Council for Academic Freedom and Academic Standards.

Halsey, A.H. (1992a) *Opening Wide the Doors of Higher Education*, NCE Briefing No. 6, London: National Commission on Education.

Halsey, A.H. (1992b) *The Decline of Donnish Dominion*, Oxford: Oxford University Press.

Kerr, C. (1995) *The Uses of the University*, Cambridge: Harvard University Press, (4th edition).

Kogan, M., Moses, I. and El-Khawas, E. (1994) *Staffing Higher Education: Meeting New Challenges*, London: Jessica Kingsley Publishers.

Leavis, F.R. (1972) *Nor Shall My Sword: Discourses on Pluralism, Compassion and Social Hope*, London: Chatto & Windus.

Miller, H. (1995) 'States, economies and the changing labour process of academics: Australia, Canada and the United Kingdom', in J. Smyth (ed.) *Academic Work: The Changing Labour Process in Higher Education*, Buckingham: SRHE/Open University Press, 40–59.

National Commission on Education (1993) *Learning to Succeed: Report of the Paul Hamlyn Foundation National Commission on Education*, London: Heinemann.

Newson, J. and Buchbinder, H. (1988) *The University Means Business*, Toronto: Garamond Press.

Nixon, J. (1995a) 'The university as a place of learning: perspectives on the 'quality' debate', in P. Carrotte and M. Hammond (eds) *Learning in Difficult Times: Issues for Teaching in Higher Education*, Sheffield: Committee of Vice-Chancellors and Principals, Universities' and Colleges' Staff Development Agency (UCOSDA), 46–54.

Nixon, J. (1995b) 'Teaching as a profession of values', in J. Smyth (ed.) *Critical Discourses on Teacher Education*, London: Cassell, 209–18.

Nixon, J. (1996) 'Professional identity and the restructuring of Higher Education', *Studies in Higher Education*, 21(1): 5–16.

Nixon, J., Martin, J., McKeown, P. and Ranson, S. (1996) *Encouraging Learning: Towards a Theory of the Learning School*, Buckingham: Open University Press.

Nixon, J., Martin, J., McKeown, P. and Ranson, S. (forthcoming) *The New Professionalism*. Buckingham: Open University Press.

Nixon, J. and Rudduck, J. (1994) 'Professionalism, judgement and the inspection of schools', in D. Scott (ed.) *Accountability and Control in Educational Settings*, London: Cassell.

Opacic, S. (1994) 'The student learning experience in the mid-1990s', in S. Haselgrove (ed.) *The Student Experience*, Buckingham: The Society for Research into Higher Education and Open University Press 157–68.

Parry, G. (1995) 'England, Wales and Northern Ireland', in P. Davies (ed.) *Adults in Higher Education: International Perspectives on Access and Participation*, London: Jessica Kingsley Publishers, 102–33.

Piper, D.W. (1994) *Are Professors Professional?* London: Jessica Kingsley Publishers.

Robbins (1963) *Higher Education* ('The Robbins Report') Report of the Committee appointed by the Prime Minister under the Chairmanship of Lord Robbins. 1961–3, London: HMSO.

Scott, T. (1995) *The Meanings of Mass Higher Education*, Buckingham: The Society for Research Into Higher Education and Open University Press.

Smith, B. and Brown, S. (1995) 'A manifesto for research, teaching and learning', in B. Smith and S. Brown (eds) *Research Teaching and Learning in Higher Education*, London: Kogan Page, 187–90.

Snow, C.P. (1993) *The Two Cultures*, Cambridge: Cambridge University Press.

Steneck, N.H. (1994) 'Ethics and the aims of universities in historical perspective', in M.N.S. Sellers (ed.) *An Ethical Education: Community and Morality in the Multicultural University,* Oxford: Berg, 9–20.

Trilling, L. (1966) *Beyond Culture: Essays on Literature and Learning*, London: Secker & Warburg.

Winter, R. (1995) 'The university of life plc: the "industrialisation" of higher education?', in J. Smyth (ed.) *Academic Work: The Changing Labour Process in Higher Education*, Buckingham: SRHE/Open University Press, 129–43.

7

PROFESSIONAL DISINTEGRATION?

The case of law

Gerard Hanlon and Joanna Shapland

THE LEGAL PROFESSIONS AND THE MARKET FOR LEGAL WORK

What impression does legal work conjure up? Is it the courtroom, with lawyers resplendent in gowns and wigs, passionately arguing the merits of the case? Is it the solicitor's office, the solicitor sitting behind a large mahogany desk, a framed practising certificate on the wall, patiently explaining the mechanisms of making a will? Is it the City firm of solicitors advising on another corporate take-over, in altogether more modern office surroundings, with atrium, plants and soft-toned furnishings, yet with the legal tomes carefully displayed? All those images are those of the professional lawyer. They all exist. Yet the vast majority of legal services are in effect a free market – they do not have to be provided by a qualified professional. The amount of legal business reserved to qualified legal professionals is very small (appearing in certain courts and a small amount of paper transactions). It is perfectly legal for your neighbour to advise you over the garden fence on your dispute with your holiday company or on your company's legal problems – whether it is wise for you to rely on that advice is the essence of the professional's claim on the market.

Essentially, the legal market in England and Wales has always been relatively deregulated (far more so than in many other countries, though Scandinavia is even more deregulated). The interesting change in the last ten years or so has been the shake-up within the legal professions, the encroachment (or apparent encroachment) of other professions, and the increasing ambiguity as to which professional should deliver management advice and services to companies (accountants? lawyers? management consultants?). It is interprofessional change, as much as (or more than) change between services delivered by professionals and services delivered by others which is significant. On top of this interprofessional change lie the stresses caused by increasing consumerism and increasing legislative/ government/quango intervention within the governance of the professional legal bodies. In the legal world we are not seeing the end of the professions, in terms of the abolition of professionals or all work being diverted to non-professionals (unless computers are non-professionals!), but we are seeing disquiet about the extent of change being forced on the dominant professionals within the professional legal domain.

By this point in the chapter, it would be expected that we would have addressed the question of what does a 'professional' mean in this respect. We are taking professionals to be members of associations which set entry standards, encourage certain standards of professional behaviour, receive complaints, take disciplinary action and, increasingly, actively monitor their members' behaviour in the workplace. Note this is not a definition couched primarily in terms of self-regulation. This is because the legal professions have always been shaped by the law and legislation (Abel-Smith and Stevens, 1967). What is more recent is the introduction of quangos with legislative backing, situated in terms of regulation between statutory means of regulation and the professional bodies, and which are engaged in making the professional associations take on certain tasks. Elsewhere, we have called these quangos 'intermediate regulators' (Shapland, 1995). Examples are the Securities and Investment Board and the Lord Chancellor's Advisory Committee on Legal Education and Conduct. Hence our problem in defining 'professional' as self-regulatory. Is a coerced self-regulatory body still a self-regulatory body? Legal professional bodies could of course refuse to take on board the duties and dictates of the quangos – but they fear that if they do, they may be subject to direct legislative control or that financial mechanisms will be used to reduce drastically their market share.

THE LEGAL PROFESSIONS IN THE 1990s

To set the scene for the 1990s, it may be helpful to describe the legal professions. The largest is clearly the solicitors – and much of the rest of this chapter focuses on the work of solicitors. The Bar, still healthy despite many rumours of its demise, remains mainly a referral profession, although certain professionals have direct access. The two traditional legal professions have now been joined by legal executives (who work almost entirely in solicitors' firms or in legal departments with employed solicitors, and so can be seen as 'junior partners') and licensed conveyancers, created when the monopoly of conveyancing for solicitors was broken. Unfortunately, this coincided with the property market crash in the late 1980s and so there are very few licensed conveyancers. Both these new professions have their own professional associations and behave like model, modern self-regulatory professions. Indeed many of their innovations have been taken up by the more traditional bodies (Allaker and Shapland, 1994a).

Our data for this chapter come from two sources. The first is a survey of professions, which focused on professional associations and hence the view from the centre of the profession. We collected documents and written material from professional associations as varied as those representing architects, social workers, accountants (chartered and certified), barristers, psychologists, general practitioners, solicitors, patent agents, surveyors, legal executives, actuaries, chemical engineers and licensed conveyancers. We then interviewed senior officials from the national association about their views and the association's policy on regulation which encourages good practice and competition (see Allaker and Shapland, 1994a; 1994b).

The second study is a national survey of solicitors' firms comprised of two partners or more and engaged in commercial legal work (Hanlon, 1995: table 7.1). This study focused on firm structure, marketing, views of senior personnel about working with other professionals and training and career structures. This survey was sent out to around six hundred firms engaged in the area of commercial law. These firms were chosen on the basis of what was found in legal directories. We took as our survey population all those firms which stated they were engaged in providing commercial law as part of their legal services range, and randomly sampled one in ten firms. There are flaws in adopting such a strategy (for example, not all firms providing these services are to be found in these directories, different directories have different entries for the same firms, firms obviously have an interest in boosting their profile in these directories which are sometimes viewed as a means of advertising). However, despite these drawbacks we feel that the survey provides an accurate reflection of what is occurring in the 'business affairs' end of the legal profession. The response rate was 33 per cent giving us roughly 200 responses. The survey was followed up with approximately twenty-one long semi-structured interviews with senior partners in firms throughout England. These interviews addressed issues such as marketing, organisational control, promotion, client behaviour, interprofessional rivalry and so on.

In order to give a truly comprehensive view of law, this chapter would have to examine a number of professions: solicitors, barristers, judges, legal executives, licensed conveyancers. However, given the spatial constraints involved in any chapter this is clearly not possible. Thus we will concentrate on the solicitors' profession. Such concentration needs to be justified. We consider that solicitors give us a real insight into how the whole legal arena is developing, as they are now the dominant branch of the profession, after almost a century of trying to climb out from under the control of the Bar and the Bench (Abel-Smith and Stevens, 1967; Glasser, 1990). A second and possibly more important reason for concentrating on solicitors is that many of the issues addressed in this book – interprofessional rivalry, managerialism, consumer behaviour, organisational settings for professional employment – have impacted most noticeably (although not exclusively) on solicitors in the legal professions area. We intend to examine some of these issues.

The chapter analyses the increasing fragmentation of the solicitors' profession. It will suggest that, on a whole range of criteria, the profession is splitting into two (and possibly more) quite separate hemispheres. These criteria include areas such as client size, firm size, work performed, professional-client interaction and form of professional regulation. This is not a new proposition. Heinz and Laumann (1982) have convincingly argued the same as regards the USA. In the UK, Abel-Smith and Stevens (1967), Offer (1981) and Miles (1984) have also highlighted that, historically, the solicitors' profession has been fragmented. For example, London solicitors sided with the Bar and opposed the decentralisation of the higher courts away from London because they would lose agency revenue as a result. However, recent trends towards fragmentation appear to be both more marked than previously and accompanied by an altogether different professional environment to the one that has existed for the past fifty years or so (see Perkin, 1989; Hanlon, 1994; 1996c for the professions generally and Abel, 1989; Thomas, 1992; Sherr, 1994, for law in particular). This new environment encourages professional competition, the merging of professional jurisdictions and entrepreneurialism amongst professions in a way that was frowned upon in the past (see Carr-Saunders and Wilson, 1933; Marshall, 1939; Wilensky, 1964 for an examination of the past). A number of areas within this fragmentation process will be analysed in order to highlight this trend.

Firm size and the producer–consumer relationship

Whilst not as concentrated as accountancy (see Hanlon, chapter 8 of this volume), the solicitors' profession is dominated by a small number of large firms. For example, in 1991–2 the largest thirty-six firms or 1 per cent of all firms (26 partners or more) accounted for 41 per cent of fees for those firms registered with the Law Society. In contrast, firms with five partners or less (80 per cent of firms) earned a mere 25 per cent of total legal fee income (Law Society, 1994). Hence economic power varies greatly as one moves through the profession from the small to the large organisations. Such a trend was reiterated by a recent survey. Seven per cent of sole practitioners were estimated to be operating at a loss in 1995, whilst median profits per partner ranged from £29,000 for sole practitioners to £61,000 for partners in firms of 11–25 partners (firms with more than 25 partners were excluded from the study – see *Gazette*, 1995). This economic power means that a limited number of firms dominate the legal services labour market. This dominance is reflected in our survey of firms engaged in selling commercial law services. Four per cent of our sample of firms

Table 7.1 Proportions of firms employing assistants by partners (%)

Number of Partners	_____	Number of assistants					
	0	1–10	11–20	21–40	41–100	100–250	251+
2–10	44.5 (53)	55.5 (66)					
11–20	6.7 (1)	46.7 (7)	46.7 (7)				
21–40	6.1 (2)	9.1 (3)	27.3 (9)	45.5 (15)	12.1 (4)		
41–100	7.7 (1)				38.5 (5)	46.2 (6)	7.7 (1)
101+						50.0 (2)	50.0 (2)

(Figures in brackets represent number of firms)

employed 29.3 per cent of all partners, 63 per cent of all trainees, and 75 per cent of all assistants.

In commercial law a small number of firms appear to be the training ground for future solicitors. It has been suggested that the recent introduction of the Legal Practice Course was a reflection of this fact. The Legal Practice Courses have been accused of mirroring the images of commercial law rather than law in a broader sense (Moorhead and Cushley, 1995).

As Table 7.1 highlights, it is also the case that these larger firms have higher leverage ratios (partner to staff ratios), which can be seen as a proxy for profitability levels (Morris and Pinnington, 1994). If we compare the leverage ratio of partners to all staff in our complete sample, it works out at 3.6 staff for every one partner, whereas if we concentrate on those firms with over fifty-five partners the figure increases to 4.7 staff to every partner. Such a change reinforces the point indicated earlier that the larger the firm the greater its profitability and/or leverage ratio. This fact leads one to assume that large law firms may be qualitatively different to their smaller counterparts in terms of their organisational structure and control. Such an assumption is argued throughout the rest of this chapter. Another factor which supports this proposition is their relationship with their clients.

Cain (1983) has suggested that in the area of law the producer (i.e. the lawyer) is often the dominant partner within the 'producer–client' relationship. Keat and Abercrombie (1991) have posited that one of the significant shifts of the 1980s has been a move away from professional dominance in a whole range of areas, including professional–client relations. Likewise, Hanlon (1994) has argued that for accountancy there has certainly been a shift in the power relationship between large accountancy firms and large clients. In law many of the trends which affected accountancy are now beginning to emerge; for example, tendering for work, 'beauty parades', and the growth in the legal sophistication of large clients. All of this indicates a change in the nature of at least some professional–client relations. This change is usually based at the large firm end of the market, due to the legally conversant client base of these law firms. It is overwhelmingly the large law firms that have the large clients, as can be seen from Table 7.2.

Table 7.2 Types of client base (%)

Law firm size	Large organisations	Medium organisations	Small organisations/ individuals
Top 13	61.5	38.5	
20–54 partners	17	78.7	4.3
Small firms	7.9	30.5	59.8

Given that our survey addressed those firms operating in the commercial law sphere, the importance of the individual client will be less than if we had surveyed all law firms, including those in the criminal law field where the individual client is the norm. Hence what has happened at the large firm end of the commercial law market is even further removed from what non-commercial lawyers experience – indicating the increased likelihood of fragmentation in the profession.

Large clients are now powerful within the professional–client relationship and they are increasingly demanding more and more from law firms in terms of costs, service, specialisation, etc. Flood (1991) has shown how powerful business clients seek to shape the professional–consumer relationship in their interest. What emerges from his insightful portrayal is a picture of constant struggle between the different parties to a conflict. There are four parties in the contest – two antagonists and two sets of lawyers – and two types of conflict (the antagonist and his or her lawyers versus the opposition and between each antagonist and his or her lawyers). How these conflicts are resolved is a matter for negotiation between all the parties; it is not simply a matter of the professionals telling their clients what is possible – the clients have a very real and powerful input. This view of clients as players was highlighted in interviews with partners of law firms in our own work:

> The pressure (from clients) is to contain and establish some boundaries to client financial commitment wherever this can be done. This means taking an intelligent position on either fixed fee – you know we're doing a lot more fixed fee work now – or at least putting a cap on fees so that we're accepting a degree of risk if the work goes beyond a certain level, or we're dividing a big project up into components and charging step by step . . . . one of the jobs of the in-house legal dept is to control outside suppliers and the biggest firms are able to do this with a great deal of sophistication. They know exactly what is involved, the reporting requirements, they know how we work, they would have been in large practice themselves.
>
> (Large law firm director)

At the other end of the spectrum – the small firm – the individual client is still relatively powerless. There are two reasons for this. One, they are unfamiliar with the law and the legal process and two, often they are very personally involved in the legal issue (for example in divorce proceedings) and thus have a heavy emotional investment in the whole process. Research on legal clients in the UK has highlighted that there is a sizeable difference between the perceptions of defendants who had previous experience of the courts and those who had not (Jackson *et al.*, 1991). Zander and Henderson (1993) have also shown that over half of defendants in criminal cases met with their barristers on the day of their trial and one in three felt they had insufficient time for consultation. This evidence is not directly comparable with the survey conducted by the authors, as it examines the criminal legal area rather than the area of civil law, however, it seems unreasonable to assume that individual clients in the civil law area, especially those engaged in the legal process for the first time, would have a much greater degree of power within the professional–client relationship than their counterparts in the field of criminal law! Such a view is reinforced by the comments of solicitors dealing with these clients:

> For example, clients come to a lawyer saying they want say a marketing agreement and you have to say fine but what you really need is a technical aid agreement as you have to establish the product before you sell it.
>
> (Small firm partner)

Hence we would argue that there is not one professional–client relationship but at least two, both entailing very different power relationships. Again such a proposition is not new; Heinz and Laumann (1982) highlighted this in the US almost fifteen years ago.

Areas of work and firm size

As one would expect, given that clients differ across law firms depending upon firm size, the type of work performed by a firm in the area of commercial law also varies. In the survey 80 per cent of respondents indicated that they had a departmental structure (the figure for the complete solicitors' profession would obviously be much smaller). Table 7.3 indicates the areas of law covered in each department by the size of firm.

The largest firms operate in the fields dominated by corporations (for example, financial services, banking, tax), whereas smaller practices work with individual clients in areas like conveyancing, family law, and so on. There is also an intermediate group of firms that operate with both sets of clients. The very largest law firms appeared from the questionnaire survey to have no individual clients. Interviews have highlighted that if these firms have any individual clients, they are either executives of corporate clients or very wealthy individuals and they are handled by a separate

110

Table 7.3 The kinds of departmental work areas (%)

	Total sample	Small firms	20–55 partners	Top 13 firms
Litigation	75.5	70.3	100	100
Commercial	55.2	49.4	100	100
Property	38.3	11.7	92	100
Personal law	33	41.2	15.0	
Conveyancing	32.3	43.8	5.0	
Private client	24.3	11.0	50	40
Trust and probate	19.2	19.6		10
Tax	9.5	0.8	14.5	70
Professional indemnity	9.5	10.2	8.4	
Other	9.5	10.1		10.0
Banking	8.4		17.5	60
Financial services	7.4		14.5	60
Intellectual property	5.1		8.5	40
Environment	4.1		8.5	30
Entertainment	3.7	1.6	8.5	10

private client department. Sometimes the large firm will recommend that they use a particular small firm or the large law firm will control a separate small firm specifically for these occasions. However, the intention appears to be to limit the number of individual clients.

In effect what this means is that solicitors in large firms deal with different areas of law, different types of clients and experience different working relations with their clients. Also, given that corporate law is a lot more large scale in its operation, these lawyers work as part of a team rather than as individuals, thereby experiencing a completely different division of labour to their legal colleagues in small firms. All of this facilitates the fragmentation of the profession. Polarisation appears to exist at the level of firm size, client size, professional-client relationship, areas of law worked in and experience of the division of labour. Such a process of fragmentation is further reinforced by way in which income is earned by law firms.

A standardised versus individualised service – Images of the future?

The difference in power between consumers impacts upon the form of service given to clients. Essentially, there may be a polarisation in service provision, i.e. the service to the small individual client may be standardised whereas the one provided to the corporate client will be individualised. Stated so bluntly this is obviously an exaggeration of the reality. However, given that the corporate market is highly specialised, clients are powerful and competition is fierce, the large law firms sell themselves as legal service providers that can match the very special and individual needs of clients. Hence they have begun to restructure themselves. Interviews appear to highlight that the large law firms are undergoing a major restructuring. The essence of this is to become more receptive to the market. Today firms are already, or considering, organising themselves along a market-industrial sector model rather than a legal specialist one. The logic behind such restructuring is that the different legal specialists who operate in, say, the banking industry group develop an in-depth knowledge of the banking industry and are therefore more in tune with the specific, individual difficulties of clients in this industry. This is seen as a real marketing advantage over those firms who organise themselves along the traditional lines of legal specialisms where, for example, there are property lawyers, litigators, commercial lawyers, etc. in various legal specialist departments who concentrate primarily on their legal specialism rather than a market-industry sector. To sum up, it is a shift away from what is perceived to be a narrow legal specialism to a broader commercial awareness, with this awareness supposedly then informing the individually specific legal solutions provided to corporate clients. By making this shift, it is argued, one can attract clients and more non-standardised, high-profit work. Similar moves are being made by a number of professional associations themselves, particularly in the construction industry, though there is no sign of it amongst legal professional bodies. The move to market sector orientation follows prompting from members, who themselves are orienting towards clients (Allaker and Shapland, 1994a). The moves being made by large law firms reflect a more general phenomenon in professional services, particularly evident where clients are more powerful and competition is becoming fiercer.

> As a matter of strategy we have taken the view from looking at our markets and our plans for the future that sector strength is one of the ways we want to differentiate ourselves in the market. I think it is true to say that most law firms think of themselves as being skill based, we've turned that around a bit and taken the view that sector strength has all sorts of benefits for clients and for us. It enables us to align ourselves very much with the interests, networks, and the knowledge that resides in a particular sector. It means that on client work we can move faster because we're down the learning curve and don't have to learn all about left-handed widgets if we're working for the first time with a new client in that particular sector. And we've found it quite a powerful way, and a way that is intelligible to clients, of presenting and marketing ourselves.

> (Large law firm director)

At the other extreme the situation is fundamentally different. The market for most law firms is made up of individual clients. This is concentrated in a number of areas, as can be seen from Table 7.4.

112

Table 7.4 Origins of fee income within the solicitors' profession (%)

Business affairs	Commercial property	Domestic conveyancing	Family	Wills and probate	Personal injury	Crime
30	15	11	8	8	6	3–4

Source: adapted from Law Society, 1994: chart 5. (Chart does not add to 100 per cent)

Given the fact that the business affairs and commercial property markets are dominated by large firms (i.e. twenty partner plus – roughly 1 per cent of the total number of firms) and that these firms are not heavily involved in the individual client areas of law, it appears to be the case that the vast majority of law firms are selling their services in a very limited number of areas – domestic conveyancing, family law, wills and probate, personal injury, and crime. These areas are very heavily influenced by two factors – the property market and legal aid.

The collapse of the property market in the late 1980s and 1990s can almost be left unstated. Such a collapse is reflected in the size of the domestic conveyancing market for solicitors. In 1988 there were an estimated 2.25 million conveyancing transactions in England and Wales; by 1992 this figure had roughly halved (Law Society, 1994: chart 3). Not only has there been pressure on the number of transactions but there has also been a marked decline in the fee per transaction. Between 1983 and 1986 it is estimated that solicitors cut 30 per cent off conveyancing fees in light of the fact that they lost their monopoly on conveyancing with the creation of the licensed conveyancers by the state (Sherr, 1994: 6). In the mid to late 1980s such cost cutting was possibly due to the property boom, which was fuelled by the general economic boom of those years, the government drive to increase home ownership at the expense of public housing, and the one-off sale of 1.5 million local authority houses (20 per cent of the total stock) to their occupiers (Pierson, 1994: 104).

Traditionally the property market has been the mainstay of the profession (Miles, 1984; Offer, 1981), so now that it is in real trouble this indicates that the profession itself, or more accurately parts of the profession, have been facing considerable difficulties. Given that the ingredients which fuelled a one-off property boom have gone (at least for the foreseeable future), it is difficult to see an end to the conveyancing 'problem' facing solicitors. In the light of this, firms have been seeking to compete on costs, cheapening their product via technology and using non-solicitors to carry out much of the work. Here, unlike the business sector, the emphasis is on providing a cheap, standard service for customers.

The increase in our partnership is not going to come from promoting young fee earners, particularly as over the last few years we have been employing more legal executives than qualified solicitors because they're cheaper. If they have ten years experience they can do a lot better job than a two-three year qualified solicitor – they specialise. So you can't make legal executives partners, so there is going to be less to choose from, but most of our partners are going to come from the mergers we do when we open offices four, five, and six .... they (legal executives) are more suitable for the purpose. Having a legal executive doing domestic conveyancing, when that legal executive is a specialist in domestic conveyancing and nothing else, is better than putting in a new young qualified solicitor who has done six months domestic conveyancing, is going to make a lot of mistakes, keeps on asking questions, and may take two or three years to get up to a reasonable standard by which time he'll probably want £30,000 a year and bring in £50,000 in fees, it's not on. Your legal executive is going to be expecting a salary of £20–25,000, has always done that work, is likely to be able to do it very much quicker, more efficiently, etc .... and some of the legal executives have come up the hard way, either through being secretaries or doing other legal roles and because of that they know what it's like. They're streetwise whereas the qualified solicitors are not that way inclined so they (legal executives) are going to do a better job for you.

(Medium law firm director)

As if these factors were not depressing enough for the small firm end of the profession, it is being attacked on other sides as well. For example, legal aid (as with other areas of the welfare state) has been subject to restructuring over the course of the Thatcher and Major administrations. Despite growing at a rate of 17 per cent per annum (if inflation is included) over the course of the 1980s, fewer people are entitled to it today than in 1979. In 1979 72 per cent of the population was eligible for legal aid; in 1990 the figure was 47 per cent. The legal aid system is currently being radically changed by the government. The form of the system being put in place has clearly been driven substantively by cost and efficiency concerns, in contrast to the notions of solidarity and egalitarianism outlined in the creation of the scheme originally (Goreily, 1994). It appears to enshrine two notions. One is that legal aid work should be restricted to those firms that have adhered to the quality and management standards laid down by the government and that these firms should then compete for franchises to perform legal aid work. The second is that the overall budget will be capped at a figure agreed to annually by parliament (*Financial Times*, 1995).

These changes will mean that firms seek to obtain franchises by meeting certain managerial and legal criteria and then competing with each other for a limited amount of work. It has been estimated that 11,000 solicitors' offices received a legal aid cheque in 1991, yet the government wishes to operate the reformed system with around 2,000 franchises (*Gazette*, 1993). Hence firms will have to engage in relatively severe competition to participate in a scheme which has a limited budget but an increasing level of demand. This, combined with the desire of the state to limit costs per case to an average level, will mean that much of the competition amongst franchisees will be at the level of costs. Sherr *et al.* (1994) have suggested that such a prospect will encourage firms to limit their unit costs in comparison with their competitors and, therefore, will encourage these firms to provide a standardised service and avoid those areas of law that are innovative, as these latter will tend to be more expensive and more likely to be refused legal aid, thereby leaving the firm unable to recoup initial case costs. Such a trend is in direct opposition to the increasingly client-centred and individualised nature of service at the large firm end of the profession. Though we are not arguing that all services at the small firm end will show this standardisation – merely that it will form a greater proportion of their work than for large firms.

There are three other possible consequences of the proposed reforms. First, in order to make legal aid profitable it is increasingly likely that firms will specialise in it. This will exacerbate a trend which has seen 11 per cent of firms gain over 50 per cent of their fees from legal aid in 1989 (Hansen, 1992: 94). Second, added to this, is the fact that the government has sought to decouple private and publicly funded law. Hence it has argued that legal aid fees to lawyers should not match those of privately paid fees. As a result, lawyers now see legal aid work as the poor relation and the least profitable area of practice to be engaged in. In a Law Society survey 18 per cent of firms stated that legal aid work was loss making (Hansen, 1992: 91). Obviously such statistics need to be treated with caution, but the separation of fees into two groups of work – one well paid and the other less so – is further evidence of a fragmenting profession. Third, the move towards franchising also creates another difficulty for the profession. It potentially opens up areas of the legal aid budget to other non-legal groups. For example, family mediation service providers are eligible for matrimonial monies; the government is explicitly steering people towards mediation rather than the courts as a means of dealing with marital breakdown (*Gazette*, 1993) and Citizens Advice Bureaux are encouraged to compete for social welfare monies in the immigration, debt, and welfare benefits arenas. It is difficult to say what the extent and impact of this opening up will be but, whatever it is, it is likely to entail a loss of money by solicitors. All of this is in marked contrast to the previous era when solicitors were one of the main beneficiaries of the legal aid system, due to the volume of lucrative work it put their way.

What do these alterations tell us about the future of this profession? There are clearly going to be two very different experiences of work to emerge out of these changes. At the corporate client end of the legal services market change will lead to an individualised service (or at least the attempt to create a perception of an individualised service) being offered to clients. Within this format, cost will be a factor but, in order to limit the importance of cost as a factor, firms will seek to provide a non-standard commercial 'quality' product for which they can charge extra. There are obvious parallels here with the 'value versus price' debate in the construction industry. At the individual client end of the market a completely different picture is being painted. In at least two of the major areas for small firms – conveyancing and legal aid – the profession is under pressure to provide a cheaper more standardised service. The only way to do this is to attack costs – by replacing solicitors with non-professionals or technology – to lower solicitors' remuneration and/or to simplify the work process. There appears to be evidence that all three are occurring. As we shall see, this will not occur at the large client end of the profession. As one interviewee commented

> we employ legal executives for specific roles: conveyancing, matri-monial hacks, wills, but you still need the expertise of qualified solicitors, particularly for commercial work. Commercial clients do expect that they've got somebody with a good legal background and know their way around a lot of issues and certainly in our com-mercial department we wouldn't consider taking on legal executives, and even in the higher grade litigation work as well you would expect to employ a good solicitor.
>
> (Medium law firm director)

THE FUTURE: PROFESSIONALISM, LAW, AND SOCIETY

If all of the above trends are correct then we may be witnessing the emergence of two solicitors' professions. These are based on firm size, work done, sources of revenue, and client size. The future for the small firms is currently very uncertain. Their traditional markets – conveyancing and legally-aided law – are currently under pressure. If this pressure intensifies, it may well be the case that many of these organisations will cease to exist. The trend towards polarisation is increasing. Despite a decline of 15 per cent in firm numbers in the 1991–2 period, the percentage of sole practitioners increased from 34 per cent to 39 per cent as a proportion of the profession between 1985–93, whilst during the same time the number of medium sized firms declined by 7 per cent (Law Society, 1994). It is difficult to see how all of these small firms can survive if extra pressure is put on them. As stated, the most recent survey suggests 7 per cent of sole practitioners are operating at a loss. At present one in three adults consult a solicitor once every three years, usually for conveyancing

116

or wills and probate. If either of these markets is lost to other professional groups (licensed conveyancers, Citizens Advice Bureaux, or others yet to be established, such as the 'law shops' staffed by law graduates common in continental Europe) then, given current difficulties, this end of profession is in real trouble.

The larger firms face a different difficulty. These firms have witnessed exceptional growth in the past twenty years in terms of size and fees. They offer an increasingly wide range of services to organisational clients in a very entrepreneurial way and appear to have placed themselves in the position of business advisers in all things legal. So far these processes have proved beneficial to them.

However, there are dangers in this trend. If law firms become too 'creative' in the solutions they offer to their large business clients, it may well start to threaten perceptions of the stability of the current capitalist system in the UK (through a potential loss of confidence in the money markets or the valuation of major companies) and will therefore force intervention by the government (with or without the support of capital). If these 'creative' trends remain unchecked, then law firms are likely to develop a poor reputation, with the result that business may seek other forms of redress and/or contract structures. Such a process would severely damage lawyering. A similar process occurred in the last century. Business clients increasingly used arbitration from the 1850s onwards as law and the courts were deemed to be too costly, too slow, too legalistic and non-commercial, and socially an inappropriate way of dealing with commercial disputes amongst business people (Cocks, 1984). Solicitors have never been able to recapture this work and as a result London is now one of the world's great arbitration centres. If lawyers today become so creative that the outcome of legal disputes becomes totally unpredictable then business may well opt for more certain mechanisms of dispute resolution and/or contract creation. Hence law needs to be careful about how creative it can become if it is to retain the confidence of the state and/or capital.

A second potential threat to the large law firm is external. As they reposition themselves as management advisers, they increasingly enter into the realm of the accountants. In some ways this is unavoidable, as the Big Six accountancy firms increasingly encroach on lawyers' traditional turf – the most adventurous so far has been Arthur Andersen which has recently taken over a medium sized law firm.

As management advisers lawyers suffer from two disadvantages. One, lawyers are lower down the 'food chain' than other professionals (i.e. business people usually go to other professionals with a difficulty and these professionals then bring in the lawyers). So, for example, when a company becomes insolvent, tax and more general corporate work accountants are brought in first, whilst in commercial property architects and/or surveyors may be involved in the deal before or after lawyers, depending upon the client. Such a process or position in the market makes expansion as a management adviser difficult. Other professionals may seek to keep management work for themselves or professional colleagues, rather than pass it on to lawyers. Changing this will require a lot of time and effort on the part of lawyers. It will entail forcing business people to change established business practices. The second problem is size. The accountancy firms are a lot bigger than the law firms. Collectively the Big Six in the UK have an income of £2.5 billion, whereas the top twenty UK law firms share £1.6 billion between them (London Economics Ltd, 1994: 1). This means that all other things being equal, it is financially a lot easier for accountants to encroach on legal work than for lawyers to expand out of this area. To what extent size proves to be a real long-term advantage remains to be seen. However, these two problems may halt the expansion of law firms into general corporate advisers. Large law firms may be destined to play the role of relatively important niche players within the professional service/corporate adviser market.

THE LEGAL PROFESSION IN THE CONTEXT OF OTHER PROFESSIONS: IS THE END NIGH?

How does this relate to professionalism and the influence of the professions? The strange thing about legal work appears to be that, although there seem to be quite active market forces at work within the profession, splitting it into the large and the small, acting both at the level of firms and at the level of the employment of individual solicitors (an issue untouched here but see Hanlon, 1994: table 7.1), the same appears to be true in relation to the balance between professionals and non-professionals in the legal sector as well. Some professionals seem to be rising above the law of the jungle, whilst others are under severe pressure to reform or face real competition within it.

As we have seen, there are at least two separate elements emerging within the solicitors' profession. The crucial distinction between them is client behaviour. At the individual client segment of the profession, lawyers are being forced to offer a more standardised service to clients in a limited number of areas – primarily conveyancing and personal law which is often legally aided. Central to the provision of this service at the present is cost (because so much is publicly funded or funded through insurance policies). Moves towards full cost recovery in the civil courts may exacerbate this emphasis on price, rather than value. Clients come to these solicitors on the basis of personal knowledge or recommendation, due to their ignorance of the service they are purchasing (Macmillan, 1995) and the one-off nature of these services. However, the difficulty from a client perspective within this is that clients are necessarily reduced to a passive role wherein the service can only be judged primarily on non-legal issues (such as speed of response to letters). There is, therefore, a need for some form of regulation, be it professional self-regulation and/or state regulation, to protect clients from a legal profession embroiled in an increasingly competitive and cost conscious market.

Large law firms are engaged in a very different world, wherein clients are large and powerful and thereby capable of protecting themselves. At this end of the market we could possibly witness the emergence of larger multi-professional service firms made up of accountants, lawyers and others (though whilst conflict of interest rules remain as strict as they are, it is not advantageous for lawyers to concentrate provision in a very few large firms – the less contentious world of accountancy has not been so affected by conflict of interest considerations). Here there is also a need for regulation. However, it is of an entirely different sort to that mentioned above – not the protection of individual clients, but the much more problematic and nebulous task of protecting the state from large scale capital employing large professional service firms to circumvent rules and regulations laid down by the state, using 'creative' solutions to commercial problems. There is evidence that capital encourages professionals to adopt a lax approach to enforcing regulations or bend them to its advantage (for a more detailed examination of this in accountancy see Hanlon, 1996b; for an analysis of this in law see McBarnet, 1994).

The ways in which these forms of regulation can be delivered cannot be identical. The history of professional regulation in the last few years has been one in which professional associations have embraced an increasingly consumerist perspective to protect clients from their members. This has involved kitemarks, stronger requirements to inform clients of progress and remedies, and more proactive monitoring of individual practices, as well as greater compulsion towards continuing professional development (Allaker and Shapland, 1994a). It is not at all clear that this has all been motivated by self-regulation in the interests of the public at large. Some has clearly been government inspired or threatened. Some has been a deliberate intention to raise and declare standards to distinguish the professional more clearly from current competitors (for example, other conveyancers, though these are not real threats) and possible future competitors who are not qualified solicitors. None the less, such regulation has not only been achieved, but has become internalised as the proper activity of professional bodies.

Regulation at the large firm level is far more difficult to achieve within a self-regulated body. Leaving aside the question of whether powerful players are likely to welcome curbs on their creativity (though the difficulty of reforming auditing argues that this will be problematic), intrinsically the problem is to organise sufficient stability and predictability within the legal/monetary system that commercial companies (and international capital) will feel safe in trading in the UK. These 'deals' are multi-professional ones – but, as we have argued, the professions are fighting to increase their share of the cake. How then can each self-regulatory professional body separately create such a climate? Even more problematically, how can professional bodies traditionally concerned with individual professionals cope with team working in large corporate entities or large partnerships – where it is essentially a task of regulating firms and affecting firm culture, not individuals? We suspect strongly that, though it may be individual professionals who help to create such stabilising rules and regimes, they will need to be backed by the major monetary institutions and the government, not by professional associations. Professional associations will, we suspect, then support the new policies to stay in the political play. In exchange, the associations will be able to internalise the rules and regimes in their codes, as relatively cheap means of creating minimum standards for the operation of such regimes.

We have moved far out on to the narrow ledge over the precipice of futurology. Inching back, we feel we can stand firm on the increasing tensions within the undivided profession of solicitors. What is less certain is the extent to which the traditional common bonds – a similar university experience, the same professional exams, the love of networking (albeit the networks tend to be with firms similar to their own), the appeal of lawyering, the professional code and other similar claims to professionalism – are enough to keep solicitors together nominally as one profession, with one professional association. It would appear more logical to suggest that a lawyer working for a large law firm has more in common with an accountant in a Big Six firm than he or she does with a sole practitioner. Far over the other side of the precipice is the prospect of multi-professional associations for large client work, which would have the knowledge and ability to match the power of clients and states.

REFERENCES

Abel, R. (1989) 'Between market and state: The legal profession in turmoil', *The Modern Law Review* 52(3): 285–325.

Abel-Smith, B. and Stevens, R. (1967) *Lawyers and the Courts – A Sociological Study of the English Legal System 1760–1965*, London: Heinemann.

Allaker, J. and Shapland, J. (1994a) *Organising UK Professions: Continuity and Change, The Law Society Research Study 16*, London: The Law Society.

Allaker, J. and Shapland, J. (1994b) *Organising UK Professions: Information about the Professions*, Sheffield: Institute for the Study of the Legal Profession.

Cain, M. (1983) 'The general practice lawyer and the client – Towards a radical conception', in R. Dingwall and P. Lewis (eds) *The Sociology of the Professions*, London: Macmillan: 106–30.

Carr-Saunders, A.M. and Wilson, P.A. (1933, reprinted 1964) *The Professions*, London: Frank Cass & Co. Ltd.

Cocks, R. (1984) 'Victorian barristers and judges and taxation – A study in the expansion of legal work' in G. Rubin and D. Sugarman (eds) *Law, Economy and Society*, Oxon: Professional Books: 445–69.

Financial Times (1995) 'Government outlines scheme to cap legal aid', *Financial Times*, 18 May.

Flood, J. (1991) 'Doing business – The management of uncertainty in lawyers' work', *Law and Society Review*, 25(1): 41–72.

Gazette (1993) 'Reading the small print', *Gazette*, 90(15): 23–4.

Gazette, (1995) 'A battle for profit', *Gazette*, 92(41): 23–4.

Glasser, C. (1990) 'The legal profession in the 1990s – Images of change', *Legal Studies* 10(1): 1–11.

Goreily, T. (1994) 'Rushcliffe fifty years on – The changing role of civil legal aid within the Welfare State', *Journal of Law and Society*, 21(4): 545–66.

Hanlon, G. (1994) *The Commercialisation of Accountancy – Flexible Accumulation and the Transformation of the Service Class*, Basingstoke: Macmillan.

Hanlon, G. (1995) 'A fragmenting profession? – Lawyers, the market, and significant others'. Paper presented at the Third Annual Conference ('Liberating Professions: Shifting Boundaries') of the Institute for the Study of the Legal Profession, University of Sheffield.

Hanlon, G. (1996a) 'Law and the market – Relationships as law's core'. Paper presented at 'Economists' Club' seminar, Institute for the Study of the Legal Profession, University of Sheffield, 4 January.

Hanlon, G. (1996b) 'Casino capitalism and the rise of the "commercialised" service class – an examination of the accountant', *Critical perspectives on Accounting* 7: 339–63.

Hanlon, G. (1996c) 'Re-regulation, professionalism and commercialisation', *Teoria Sociologica*, 6.

Hansen, O. (1992) 'A future for legal aid?', *Journal of Law and Society* 19(1): 85–100.

Heinz, J.P. and Laumann, E.O. (1982) *Chicago Lawyers – The Social Structure of the Bar*, New York: Russell Sage Foundation, New York and American Bar Association.

Jackson, J., Kilpatrick, R. and Harvey, C. (1991) *Called to Court – A Public View of Criminal Justice in Northern Ireland*, Belfast: SLS Publications.

Keat, R. and Abercrombie, N. (1991) *Enterprise Culture*, London: Routledge.

Law Society (1994) *Directory of Solicitors and Barristers*, London: The Law Society.

London Economics Ltd. (1994) *The Competitive Advantage of Law and Accountancy in the City of London*, London: Corporation of London.

McBarnet, D. (1994) 'Legal creativity: Law, capital and legal avoidance' in M. Cain and C.B. Harrington (eds) *Lawyers in a Postmodern World*, Buckingham: Open University Press: 73–84.

Macmillan, L. (1995) *Client Care – A Report of a Survey on the Client Care Provided by the Solicitors in Scotland*, Glasgow: Scottish Consumer Council.

Marshall, T.H. (1939) 'The recent history of professionalism in relation to social structure and social policy', *Canadian Journal of Economics and Political Science* 5: 325–40.

Miles, M. (1984) 'Eminent practitioners – The new visage of country practitioners 1750–1800' in G. Rubin and D. Sugarman (eds) *Law, Economy and Society*, Oxon: Professional Books: 470–503.

Moorhead, R. and Cushley, D. (1995) *Quality and Access: A Blueprint for the Future – Response to the Lord Chancellor's Advisory Committee on Legal Education and Conduct Review of Legal Education*, Nottingham: Trainee Solicitors' Group.

Morris, T.J. and Pinnington, A.H. (1994) 'Firms of solicitors', *The Management of Professional Service Firms: A Survey of Policy and Practice*, 1, London: Centre for Organisational Research, London Business School.

Offer, A. (1981) *Property and Politics 1870–1914*, Cambridge: Cambridge University Press.

Perkin, H. (1989) *The Rise of Professional Society*, London: Routledge.

Pierson, C. (1994) 'Continuity and discontinuity in the emergence of the "Post-Fordist" Welfare State' in R. Burrows and B. Loader (eds) *Towards A Post-Fordist Welfare State?* London: Routledge: 95–113.

Shapland, J. (1995) 'Self-regulation of the professions – Coercion or free choice?'. Paper presented at seminar: *Regulating the Professions*, University of Strathclyde, Glasgow.

Sherr, A. (1986) 'Lawyers and clients – The first meeting', *The Modern Law Review*. 49(3): 323–57.

Sherr, A. (1994) 'Come of age', *The International Journal of the Legal Profession*, 1(2): 3–12.

Sherr, A., Moorhead, R. and Paterson, A. (1994) 'Assessing the quality of legal work: Measuring processes', *International Journal of the Legal Profession* 1(2): 135–58.

Thomas, P.A. (1992) 'Thatcher's will', *Journal of Law & Society*, 19(1).

Wilensky, H. (1964) 'Professionalisation of everyone', *American Journal of Sociology*, LXX(2): 137–58.

Zander, M. and Henderson, P. (1993) *The Crown Court Study*, Royal Commission on Criminal Justice Research Study 19. London: HMSO.

8

A SHIFTING PROFESSIONALISM

An examination of accountancy

Gerard Hanlon

INTRODUCTION

Any analysis of the changing nature of professionalism in the 1990s is incomplete without incorporating accountancy. This chapter will examine the growth and changing nature of accountancy over the past decade or so in the UK. Accountants appear to have been one of the main beneficiaries of the 1980s. For example, between 1985 and 1989 the largest eight accountancy firms (mergers have since reduced this number to six) grew at rates of between 112 per cent and 206 per cent in terms of their fee income and between 24 per cent and 73 per cent in terms of staff (Hanlon, 1994: table 2.2); over the course of the whole decade, the Big Six expanded their fee income sixfold (London Economics Ltd, 1994: 23). In 1993 the Big Six accountancy firms earned £2.5 billion between them (London Economics Ltd, 1994: 1). These six international firms now dominate the accountancy market internationally, controlling 56 per cent of leading company audits, or 74 per cent of the audit market in terms of total company sales, or 65 per cent of company audits in terms of assets (Leyshon *et al.*, 1987: table 3).

Whatever statistics one uses it is evident that these firms control the international accounting market. To understand what is happening to the profession it is important to examine the organisational and control structures of these firms. Leyshon *et al.* (1987: i) have argued that the emergence of these firms has polarised the profession in terms of practice size, client size and skill. To exaggerate, the large firms serve international and national clients in a changing accounting market and the small and medium size firms serve individuals, small and medium clients in a more limited number of areas. Such a hypothesis appears to be backed up by the literature (see Counsell, 1988, Briston, 1989, Davis *et al.*, 1993, Hanlon, 1994). In the light of this polarisation it is the intention of this chapter to concentrate on those 'elite' firms that appear to have altered their organisational and control structures to benefit from the shifting market for accountancy services. Concentrating on the Big Six is also significant in

123

another sense because between them they employ roughly 30,000 professionals in the UK (London Economics Ltd, 1994: table 8). To highlight some of the issues this chapter will analyse a number of areas: professional-client interaction, marketing, interaction of the market with the organisational structure of the firm and the individual accountant's career, and finally, the changing nature of professionalism at a societal level.

What follows is based upon fieldwork carried out by the author between 1990 and 1993 in the USA and Ireland. This research was both qualitative and quantitative. It involved the interviewing of 55 accountants at different levels within the Big Six and the surveying of 400 accountants in Ireland and 250 Irish accountants overseas. The response rates to these two questionnaires were 30 per cent and 40 per cent respectively. Although there are differences between the Big Six in Ireland, the USA and the UK it is still valid to use the Irish and American experiences to inform a chapter about Britain as the Big Six have increasingly moved towards 'world firm' strategies in order to homogenise the level of service internationally (Hanlon, 1994: 65–74).

FIRM SIZE AND THE PRODUCER–CONSUMER RELATIONSHIP

As suggested earlier, the Big Six international accountancy firms deal with large national or multinational clients. The traditional idea about professional service provision is that the professional controls the interaction with the client and translates the clients' desires into a professional meta-language and/or explains to clients what is possible in their situation (for a general example, see Hughes (1963); see Cain (1983) for an example of this in law, and Porter (1990) for an account of this in medicine). Such a view is now being challenged in a number of areas (see Flood (1991) for an account of how powerful clients shape the professional–client relationship in law; see Hanlon and Shapland's critique of this assumption as regards law in chapter 7, see Hanlon (1994: 107–52) for a detailed explanation of the weakness in this approach as regards accountancy).

This chapter will highlight how the professional–client relationship has impacted upon the organisational structures and the career paths of accountancy firms and accountants. When discussing clients one has to separate the informed from the uninformed consumer. Abercrombie and Keat (1991) have suggested that one of the key changes of the 1980s has been the decline of professional dominance in the professional–client interaction. For accountancy, there appears to be a great deal of truth in this but it is dependent upon the size of the client firm (see Hanlon and Shapland in chapter 7 for a similar argument as regards law). Thus one senior manager in the USA commented

124

I would say it's all over the board (that we learn from clients). I would say many companies, especially the larger ones, you have very competent in-house personnel and they are able to define their needs and often times they'll bring us in for when they have got an additional project and they just don't have the manpower in-house to do it and then you have other companies who are growing extremely quickly and that have not caught up to their growth and do not have the expertise in-house and all of a sudden the dollars are very large. They will say what do we need? Help us . . . they don't even know sometimes that they need help and a lot of times we're able to gather that information while we're working out on the audit and because we've come so close to the company we understand exactly what they're doing and where they're located, where they're paying tax, where they're not paying tax and we're able to spot a lot of issues for them. That's how we're able to get a lot of technical work. The audit process in some instances is a marketing exercise for us.

(Jim Spangler, Big Six senior manager, USA)

As the quotation above indicates, clients are not an homogenous group. Some are knowledgeable and therefore active whereas others are less knowledgeable and more inclined to use their professional advisers in the traditional manner, however, even here it is expected that after they have experienced significant growth they will develop the expertise to behave actively. If clients are knowledgeable it means that they can treat the accounting services (or at least elements of accounting services) in a way similar to other commodities. This has led to cost cutting, especially in the audit market, as accountancy firms seek to sell some services on the basis of cost.

I think the profession is trying to do something about it (cost cutting, known as low balling within the profession). I know it's definitely happened in the UK and the USA, I don't know what the situation is in Europe, in France or Italy where the legal structures in terms of the requirements for the audit are different. But unfortunately when people became cost discerning the audit did become a commodity in some people's eyes at least for a while. It was just a necessity, anyone can do it, it's like having your windows washed they'll pay the lowest fee and I think all the professions have tried very hard to re-educate people but that has not been the case with the audit because there is a lot of by-product to an audit that is a lot of value added. But yeah, yeah people continue to just take the lowest price for something that legally has to be done so you do have to look around for other areas of work.

(Andrea Simpson, Big Six senior manager, USA)

There are two issues that arise here. One, the audit is now a cost sensitive product in a way that does not appear to have existed in the past. Previously, clients were more interested in the spatial spread of a firm and their long-term relationship with the practice than they were in price (Jones, 1981). Today, for accountancy services as a whole, it is still of great importance to a client that the firm has a wide geographical network and/or is a member of the Big Six but for the audit market, price is increasingly important (NERA, 1992: table 3.13). Two, within accountancy there has been a shift in terms of prestige and financial reward away from auditing towards other value added areas as the audit market stagnates and is subject to cost cutting. It is to the area of market change that we now turn.

A SHIFTING MARKET FOR ACCOUNTANCY SERVICES

Perhaps the most noticeable change within accountancy has been the shift away from the audit towards other services. At the start of the 1980s the audit contributed 70 per cent to the Big Six's total fee income. By 1987 it contributed 52 per cent to the Big Six fee income in the UK and by 1993 this figure had declined to 39.4 per cent despite the fact that in the intervening six years audit fees expanded by 86 per cent up from £542 millions to just over £1 billion (see London Economics Ltd, 1994: figure 1, figure 2 and table 11). Obviously the real growth areas were elsewhere. The areas that experienced the greatest expansion were insolvency (292 per cent), tax (192 per cent) and management services (163 per cent) (London Economics Ltd, 1994: table 11). A similar trend occurred in other EU states as the audit declined in importance (NERA, 1992: table 3.7).

This lunge towards stagnation and decline in terms of total contribution to Big Six fees coincided with the increased propensity of clients to threaten to change their auditors and hence to encourage price competition. In the early 1990s it was estimated that 4 per cent of clients shifted auditors annually within the Big Six, a figure that was increasing (NERA, 1992: 89). Although the figure of 4 per cent appears to be low there is also evidence to suggest that clients were threatening to change auditors if their demands were not met (Hanlon, 1996b). Given the fact that 56 per cent of the EU's largest client firms spend 80 per cent of their *total* expenditure on the accountancy firms that perform the audit (NERA, 1992: table 3.10) it is likely that such threats proved very persuasive. As suggested earlier, the audit appears to be used as a mechanism by which other work is gained (see the Jim Spangler and Andrea Simpson quotations above). Not only is this non-audit work growing but it is also more profitable (NERA, 1992: 77). As a senior manager in a Big Six firm commented:

Yeah I think it clearly is [tax is value added]. I think while our services are included within the financial statements and we get whatever they get on the audit for that but in the tax planning and tax return clients' work our realisation tends to be better than general audit. So yeah, I mean tax is definitely one of the value added services we can give our clients. In many instances we would realise 100 per cent, generally not on clients' work tax return preparation but specific consulting projects and tax planning, yeah.

(Jim Spangler, Big Six senior manager, USA)

In contrast to this auditing has a poor realisation record:

No very rarely [do we realise 100 per cent of the audit fee]. I think they have a specific break even point and after that is profit for the partnership. So that's the thing you're working at one specific level – the audit. I believe that generally it isn't a profitable area in the overall fee generation of an organisation like a Big Six firm – consultancy, tax, these are profitable.

(Phil Doyle, Big Six senior manager, USA)

However, all of this is not to say that the audit is unimportant to the Big Six. The audit is often the gateway for the Big Six to prove their profitability potential to a client organisation. In order to do this the Big Six have begun to alter what it means to be trustworthy.

What professionals sell to clients is primarily technical assistance and trust or reputation. Incongruously, this trustworthiness is purchased but is important nevertheless. Individual or small organisational clients with little professional expertise of their own purchase services on the basis of either personal recommendation or previous experience (see Macmillan, 1995: table 27 where 78 per cent of solicitor clients used one of these two methods; Hanlon, 1994: 52–6 outlines a similar process in accountancy). Likewise with major well informed clients work comes in on the basis of relationships and personal knowledge:

Developing a good relationship, there are certain clients that don't know what they're doing and get frustrated and you have to be able to get the information from them, and they'll say I don't know what it is or it doesn't exist and you have to be able to push them to do that additional level of work without getting them mad at you, and I think there is kind of an art to that, and I think that if you can do that effectively then the next step up should be that you're a good marketer because you've exhibited interpersonal skills and pre- sumably those interpersonal skills should allow you to do marketing. I mean the most important thing in marketing is getting to know the person, the client, what their needs are, once you do that selling it should be the easy part of it, especially on the tax side because we should be able to show them they can get a benefit from it. So it's really developing the relationship with the client.

(Jim Spangler, Big Six senior manager, USA)

Even when it comes to relationships with other professionals, accountants are seeking to establish a degree of personal contact and to establish a strong link:

> In a case of a person like me, I do a lot of litigation work and it's all one-shot deals, no annual clients like an audit would be, I am going out there now to speak on law and accounting related topics, to take lawyers to lunch, to make sure that on those engagements I work on I make follow-up contacts with lawyers who are my age and who will be partner about the time I am partner. We'd have good solid relationships and they'd see me in action and when they need somebody they'd call me.

(Debra Heinz, Big Six manager, USA)

What exactly are these relationships judged on? In the past professional relationships were supposed to be disinterested or they were supposed to have a social service ethos (see Marshall, 1939; Wilensky, 1964; Hughes, 1963). However, today this ethos has been replaced with a more commercialised value system. In order to develop strong relationships that will bring in new business one has to prove to one's clients that one can improve their financial position in some respect. In accountancy during the 1980s and 1990s this was done in three ways: (1) via moving into other markets such as tax, consultancy, etc. (2) it was also done through redefining the purpose of the audit, and (3) through redefining who the client for the audit was. Having examined the shift in accountancy's market away from auditing, we need to examine the other two propositions.

REDEFINING THE PURPOSE OF THE AUDIT

The audit came to be seen by accountants as a means of providing the client with more information about their control systems. One example of this was the introduction of the management letter in the 1980s whereby accountants provided clients with advice on how to improve their control systems and clients were used as a feedback mechanism for assessing individual accountants (Hanlon, 1994: 138). Such policies redefined the role of the audit. It was no longer a public watchdog role but one of management adviser.

REDEFINING WHO THE CLIENT FOR THE AUDIT IS

Coinciding with the shift in the role of the audit was an alteration in who the primary client was. Throughout the 1980s the client was defined as the senior management personnel within the large client organisations *not* the shareholders, the state, or the public.

> It (the audit) is very much an after the event situation. You're constantly hassling people to do something. An audit is not something that anybody [*not* even shareholders nor the public!] wants but they have no choice in the matter. They have to have it and the attitude of the client can be, I mean they can really get it across at all levels, they can take that attitude with the partner down and by the time they reach us it's sometimes impossible to deal with them.
>
> (Jane O'Driscoll, Big Six senior manager)

This is in marked contrast to who the client was in the eyes of both the shareholders and the public (Humphrey *et al.*, 1992). It is also in marked contrast to an image of professionalism that was dominant throughout the bulk of the post-war period (Hanlon, 1994). This shift in the market for accounting services, the role of the audit and the redefining of the client has altered the profession in terms of which areas are deemed to be the most prestigious.

PRESTIGE AND ACCOUNTANCY SPECIALISMS

As outlined, neither the accountancy profession nor its client base are homogenous. This fragmentation of the profession comes in a number of forms, for example, large firms versus small firms, industry based accountants versus those in practice, 'commercialists' versus the more traditional professionals, and so on. This last segmentation is the one of interest to us and it reflects the changing nature of prestige within the profession. To sum up, this divide is based around those accountants that feel professionals should be commercially oriented rather than adhere to a more traditional professional ideal, and those who adhere to this traditional ideal (although in reality this ideal was never attained).

There are a number of dimensions on which these two segments differ. In particular three appear to be important (Hanlon, 1996b). One, in the new growth areas it is felt that to give 'sound managerial advice', to be profitable, and to work vigorously to fulfil your client's requirements are the essence of professionalism:

> One, I suppose, and one should never ignore it, a firm like ours is a commercial organisation and the bottom line is that. In other words unless an individual is going to be able to contribute to enlarging the cake they really have little or no chance . . . first of all the individual must contribute to the profitability of the business. In part that is bringing in new business but essentially profitability is based upon the ability to serve existing clients well.
>
> (Peter O'Neill, Big Six director)

129

In contrast to this, the social services segment of the profession stress the need to serve the public (McNeil, 1992).

Two, work activities are also viewed differently. Many accountants and clients view the audit as an expensive waste of time and resources whereas providing tax minimisation skills or some other 'new' service is deemed to be more profit driven and therefore easier to realise a full fee on and hence prestigious (see previous Jim Spangler and Jane O'Driscoll quotations). The audit is not viewed as something that will ensure the public or the shareholder's interest and is not therefore worthwhile.

Three, the relationships with clients are different. Different segments of the Big Six have different relational experiences with clients. For example, auditors are deemed to be a waste of time and an expense whereas those in other areas of the Big Six are often viewed as experts that will increase client's profitability despite the large bill. As stated, the auditors have sought to move down this 'commercial' road by writing up a management letter in order to make it appear more 'worthwhile' but this has met with only limited success. Hence auditors are seen as being of little direct use:

> In the end as well you don't really feel you're fulfilling anything (by performing an audit). All you're doing is fulfilling a legal requirement. You're not actually, there is very little benefit to the client [i.e. managers *not* shareholders or the public!] all he is doing, like he has to do it by law whereas maybe if you're in industry you'd feel money is actually being made and you're helping to make it. You're actually doing something that is real as opposed to just going in there and annoying somebody for two or three weeks and giving them a whopping bill at the end of it.
>
> (Jean Devoy, Big Six senior manager)

This shift away from the audit is in contrast to what the public wishes. The public still sees the auditors' primary function to be that of fraud detection (Humphrey *et al.*, 1992).

The reasons for these shifts are manifold. However, they are largely bound up with two processes. One, the changing nature of organisational control within the Big Six and two, recent economic restructuring and the transition from a Fordist to a 'flexible accumulation' regime. The rest of the chapter will be largely devoted to these two issues.

CHANGING NATURE OF ORGANISATIONAL CONTROL WITHIN THE BIG SIX

The Big Six have begun to alter their organisational structures in the past decade or so. This alteration reflects the changing nature of demand for their services and the decline of the audit as the main revenue generator. This restructuring entails a shift from a structure based on accounting specialism to a commercial specialist format, i.e. they are moving away from a departmental structure based on accounting specialisms such as auditing, tax, insolvency, and so on, to a more commercially oriented format wherein departments or groups are based on an industry sector approach. For example, there is a hi-tech industry sector which is made up of consultants, tax people, auditors, etc. and these individuals specialise in this industry in the belief that such specialisation will give them increased knowledge of the industry, which is then used to sell the Big Six firm initially and later on, after working for the client, other services:

> We already have groups organised on an industry basis within offices and around the firm. That's not a bad idea, these groups have auditors, tax people, consultants, and so on. I am one of the firm's leading people in publishing and I can't ever imagine wanting to know all there is about tax but I have a partner downstairs who loves taxes and who knows a lot about publishing and I can take him anywhere and our clients know they can call him. . . . I think most of our people at manager level and above are industry focused and spend most of their time on one or maybe two industries and I think our clients expect that, they've a right to expect that.
>
> (Robin Moore, Big Six partner)

Central to this organisational shift is the need to replace the unpopular low profit audit with other more commercially aware, high value added products. The Big Six are seeking to steal a march on one another by appearing to be more commercially aware than their counterparts. They believe there are marketing advantages to be gained by specialisation on industry rather than professional lines and by using the information gathered by industry specific auditors to cross-sell other services (see Jim Spangler quotation earlier, although for a different perspective see NERA, 1992). All of this means that to sell accounting services one must appear to be business-like as opposed to holding the disinterested professional ideals written about in earlier decades (see Marshall, 1939; Wilensky, 1964; Perkin, 1989).

> There is not a great deal of movement of clients and we'd argue that the best source of new work is to do your existing work well. The best way of getting new work is to have a reputation of doing work well, giving good advice, being technically sound, commercially aware or whatever.
>
> (Peter O'Neill, Big Six director)

There is also a second element to this organisational change that concerns the promotional criteria for young (and indeed older) accountants. Hanlon (1994: 107–52) has argued that there are three skill categories required in an accountant's career – technical, commercial and social.

Technical skill is basically the ability to perform the job, for example, define the audit scope, ensure the control mechanisms within the company are secure, and so on. Commercial skill is the ability to control budgets, ensure that staff perform to budgets, set the budget so that a profit is made but the fees do not appear exorbitant, put the right people on any particular job, etc. Social skills are basically the ability to bring in more business and to enlarge the cake so that the partnership can sustain you as a partner. These skills form a hierarchy so that one requires technical skills to become a senior accountant in a Big Six firm, one needs technical and commercial skills to achieve managerial status, and finally one needs all three skill elements if one is to achieve the pinnacle of success – partnership. The emergence of this hierarchy is recent. Central to it is the issue of profitability. It has led to a situation wherein seniors will 'eat time', i.e. they will not bill all the hours they have worked on a job in order to come in under the budget a partner or manager has set. Often these budgets are unrealistic but are required if the order is to be landed (see McNair, 1991):

> It is the thing I detest about my job and it is the thing that is ultimately going to drive me away from public accounting. The constant pressure to do things in less time and we have what is supposedly an iron clad rule which requires all our staff people to put all their time on time sheets, they quickly learn that that is not going to help their careers at all so our staff people don't put all their time on their time sheets. Managers more or less encourage them not to do so.
>
> (Frank Rogers, Big Six manager)

At a partnership level the capacity to make a profit is even more pronounced. Partnership is only given to those individuals that bring in more profit (see Peter O'Neill quotation earlier). Young accountants are very much aware of this need to bring in new business. Hence Debra Heinz, a Big Six manager, commented:

> I am guessing but what I see is making sure the service to the client is a business, that you are handling a block of business that supports you and all the people underneath you, you're supporting your pyramid, that you're maintaining a stable book of business, that the clients in it are revenue producing on a continuous basis, and you're able to bring in sufficient new long term business to support the people underneath you. It is not good enough just to be selling enough business just to be supporting yourself, you have to be supporting all your subordinates, and your secretary, and your file cabinets and rent. I need to be managing my business almost as an entrepreneur would.

That the Big Six have moved to an organisational format which they believe facilitates fee generation and that they have begun to assess people in this manner is no coincidence, rather it was or is part of a strategy to continue revenue expansion via giving the paying client, rather than the public, the state, the shareholders, or some social service ethic, what he or she wants or can be sold.

> Part of what motivates people is how they are going to be evaluated, how are they going to be promoted and how are they going to be compensated and historically when you work along functional lines the tax person was only interested in selling tax services and he wasn't concerned with selling auditing services and vice versa and no one was really concerned about selling consulting services. You know it was a nice thing to do from time to time but from an individual standpoint there wasn't anything to be gained really . . . but now rewarding people on how their market group does is going to encourage a lot more cross-utilisation and cross-selling.
>
> (Gary Matthews, Big Six partner)

Professionalism in this particular instance is really a business (see Hanlon and Shapland, chapter 7, for a similar account of the legal profession). The emergence of this promotional process is relatively recent. Farmar (1988) has suggested that in small accountancy practices in Ireland until the 1960s and 1970s promotion was altogether more informal. This is unsurprising given that these firms were small and partners had the opportunity to get to know and assess most individuals within the firm. Sorensen *et al.* (1973) have also demonstrated that in the 1960s young accountants were becoming more profession oriented rather than firm oriented and they were rejecting hierarchy, work standardisation, organisational loyalty, and so on, and that within partnership they suggested that young partners were less inclined to accept these things than older partners. Hence accountancy was apparently very different in its ethos thirty years ago than it is today. There is a feeling amongst young senior accountants and managers that the assessment criteria used in the 1990s is relatively new:

> Because the industry has really matured, the profession has seemed to mature, we're not growing like we used to and there is a real premium on bringing in business. I think ten years ago you could make partner without any business development as long as you were technically competent, you were here for fourteen years and you got along with your clients. Now if you've been here fourteen years, you get along with your clients and people generally like you I don't think you'll make partner.
>
> (Mike Sinclair, Big Six manager)

So why has this shift occurred recently, is it confined to accountancy and what will its impact be at a wider societal level?

GERARD HANLON

ECONOMIC RESTRUCTURING AND COMMERCIALISED PROFESSIONALISM

There has been a very significant change in the socio-economic organisation of capitalism within the Anglo-American world (and possibly beyond) in the past two decades. This transition has been given a wide variety of names – post-Fordism, post-modernism, flexible accumulation, and so on. For my purposes I will use the term flexible accumulation as outlined by Harvey (1989). The basic contention of this section of the chapter is that there has been a move from one regime of accumulation to another. A regime of accumulation has two levels – an economic mode of production and a means of social regulation. In order to understand how and why there has been an alteration we very briefly need to examine what has occurred in the past fifty to sixty years (for a more detailed description see Hanlon, 1994: 1–32; 1996a).

The regime of accumulation which has been replaced was called Fordism. Fordism existed from roughly 1930 until the mid-1970s. It entailed two fundamental features. One, it provided capital with consistently high profits over the course of the post-war boom and two, it guaranteed rising living standards to the main body of labour. These two goals were achieved via a compromise between labour and capital at an industrial and political level. To exaggerate, conflict was channelled into politics and capital was given control over the production process in return for increasing living standards and job security for labour. All of this took place against the backdrop of a move towards mass production, the growth of large heavily unionised manufacturing plants with increasing levels of productivity. The goods produced in these plants were sold to a population with a rising standard of living thereby increasing the profitability of capital.

One of the most significant consequences of this period was the segmentation of the labour market and the rise of bureaucratic control. The labour market was divided into three sections – the primary labour market, the subordinate primary market and the secondary labour market. The primary market was reserved for middle-class, professional, career oriented labour; the subordinate primary labour market was made up of male, working-class, unionised employment which was given rising living standards and long-term job security; and the secondary labour market consisted of insecure, poorly paid female and/or migrant labour. This latter market gave Fordism a degree of flexibility. Much of this employment, especially in the primary and subordinate primary sectors, was controlled via bureaucratic means, i.e. there was a fine division of labour and agreed rules and regulations were specified which, if they were adhered to, ensured long-term employment security and some measure of career progression. As suggested, the secondary sector were left out of much of this compromise.

134

At a political level there was also the creation of a welfare state. One of the key beneficiaries of this were professional employees (Hanlon, 1996a). The health, education, social security, legal aid systems, etc. all expanded rapidly and the bulk of new professional recruits entered the *public not the private* sector (see Hanlon, 1996a; Perkin, 1989; HMSO, 1971). These professionals were socialised into an employment situation wherein theoretically they were promoted on technical grounds; they were to serve the public, their salary and resources came solely from the public purse, etc. In practice many of these ideals were not adhered to: Perkin (1989) highlights how doctors, teachers, and social workers all used their power and situation to control as many resources as they possibly could. However, what appears undeniable is that these professionals justified themselves via a social service ethic. Marshall (1939: 33) argued that these professionals rejected commercialism and the market in favour of what he termed social service. In Marshall's opinion these people would have been as comfortable with socialism as capitalism provided their status and benefits remained untouched. Similar views were aired by many theorists in the post-war period (Goode, 1957; Wilensky, 1964; Hughes, 1963; Perkin, 1989). This is a very different view of professionalism to the one outlined by the accountants in this chapter.

The Fordist regime began to break down in the mid-1970s. This was primarily due to a collapse in the level of profitability. By the late 1960s profit levels for capital began to decline due to increased competition from a rebuilt Europe and Japan, the markets for many of the consumer goods which provided the bulk of profits became saturated, and finally, labour was very powerful and capable of demanding increasing concessions from capital. Thus profitability in the EU declined by 40 per cent between 1967–75 (Commission of European Communities, 1989: table 42) and in the USA a similar process occurred (Harrison and Bluestone, 1988).

As a result of these shifts capital began to alter and/or intensify some of its policies. Basically these entailed an attack on labour. Thus, spatially, capital became much more active and sought to play one region off against another in a bid to lower labour's demands, likewise plants were played off one another in order to use the most profitable plant as a benchmark for others, new policies were introduced to control and employ labour so probation periods were lengthened, firms sought to downsize and have work carried out externally whereas previously it had been done in-house, and so on. In short there was a shift towards a flexible labour market. Much of this has been outlined elsewhere (see Hanlon, 1994: 1–32; Sassen, 1991; Harvey, 1989; Harrison and Bluestone, 1988; for a more detailed discussion of these processes). All of this change was accompanied by a shift in the mode of production away from mass production of standard products to a more flexible production system wherein goods were more differentiated than under Fordism; cultural capital was increasingly purchased via products; fashions changed much quicker thereby speeding up the obsol-escence of goods, etc. (Harvey, 1989). The change in the mode of pro-duction and the economic structure required a further change in the social regulation of the labour market. This was achieved through a resegment-ing of the labour market so that the secondary labour market expanded, the subordinated primary labour market contracted and the primary labour market was radically altered. Given that we are interested in professional labour this chapter will concentrate on the last issue (but for those interested in the other two see Sassen, 1991; Harvey, 1989; Harrison and Bluestone, 1988; Murray, 1988).

How did the primary labour market alter? The most significant altera-tion within the primary labour market was that, unlike under Fordism, *the private sector was the main generator of new professional employment* (Hanlon, 1996a; Rajan, 1987; Gershuny and Miles, 1983). As highlighted earlier, occupations such as accountancy experienced enormous growth over the course of the 1980s and 1990s whilst areas such as education, health, social services and so on, experienced stagnation or relatively modest growth. One of the main reasons for this is the breakdown of the Fordist political consensus and a retreat from the ideals of the welfare state in the UK (Burrows and Loader, 1994). This ensured that the growth of the public sector slowed. In contrast to this, private sector professionals were highly sought after because in the new economic environment which was increasingly global, competitive, unstable and complex the expertise of these professionals allowed capital some element of control (Sassen, 1991: 23). For example, accountants control the finances of business empires ranging from New York to London to Hong Kong; advertisers attempt to control or influence the market; lawyers seek to structure relations between capital, and so on.

In order to access this work these professionals had to redefine what professionalism meant – they had to engage and welcome commercialism, entrepreneurialism, etc. As outlined earlier, accountants have embraced this change and used it to their advantage (lawyers appear to have done so as well, see chapter 7). This shift on the part of certain professionals has been facilitated by a broader transition within society and the emergence of an entrepreneurial culture with a subsequent downgrading of social service ethics (Abercrombie and Keat, 1991) and by the fact that this form of professionalism is the form within the primary labour market that is growing numerically. Such growth has split the service class into two categories: those that endorse this form of commercialised professionalism and the segment that thrived under Fordism. The fragmentation of the service class is real and will persist for some time. It is one of the factors in the decline of a political consensus (Savage *et al.*, 1992; Perkin, 1989). A return to any form of Fordist consensus is hampered by this transforma-tion of the social structure. These two elements of the service class derive their wealth, status and power in very different ways. The commercialised service class are intimately linked with the search for profitability and hence are likely to endorse the current regime of accumulation, their social service counterparts on the other hand derive much of their position from the expansion of the state sector and the provision of service regardless of ability to pay (Hanlon, 1994: 215–19).

At the level of individual careers does this shift matter? The answer I would suggest is yes. This transition is detrimental to members of society who have not got the commercial and social skills required to develop the contacts and networks needed to bring in new business. Hanlon (1994: 138–52) suggests that accountancy excludes members of the working class at the level of partnership because these people do not have the resources to bring in new work. These resources are social – school background, club membership, father's occupation, and so on. Hence commercialised professionalism excludes those people who are technically expert within a profession because they have not got the qualities deemed necessary to 'succeed', i.e. bring in business. In contrast the previous professional ethos supposedly valued technical ability over commercial and social ability so that (theoretically at least) any professional who was technically gifted was entitled to promotion.

CONCLUSION

What is occurring at the professional end of the labour market is simply one element within a broader level of social change. Professionals have been forced to alter their ideologies, work practices, promotional criteria, organisational structures, etc. in response to the new demands of capital. Many professionals have welcomed and benefited from this change. There is also evidence that even those professional groups which benefited most from the Fordist era and were the most entrenched in its social service value system are being forced to change. Thus doctors, educationalists, legal aid lawyers and so on, are having new organisational and control structures placed upon them and they have to respond to this via new commercial criteria (see McNulty et al., 1993; Walby, 1993; Burrage, 1992; Goreily, 1994; and chapters 5 and 6 in this volume). How exactly these professions will react to change is a moot point. It is most unlikely that they will behave in the same manner as accountants given their different histories, the way in which they interact with clients, the potential market for their services and so on. What does, however, appear clear is that the battle to set the hegemonic professional ideology for the foreseeable future is currently being fought out. How exactly this struggle finishes up will depend on the power of the professional groups concerned but, more importantly, it will also depend on the role of wider social and class forces.

REFERENCES

Abercrombie, N. and Keat, R. (1991) *Enterprise Culture*, London: Routledge.

Briston, R. (1989) 'Wider still and wider', *Accountants' Magazine*, August.

Burrage, M. (1992) 'Mrs Thatcher and deep structures', *Institute of Governmental Studies Working Paper 92–111*, Berkeley: University of California.

Burrows, R. and Loader, B. (eds) (1994) *Towards A Post-Fordist Welfare State?* London: Routledge.

Cain, M. (1983) 'The general practice lawyer and the client – Towards a radical conception' in R. Dingwall and P. Lewis (eds) *The Sociology of the Professions*, London: Macmillan, 106–30.

Commission of the European Communities (1989) *Employment in Europe*, Brussels: European Commission.

Counsell, G. (1988) 'Multidiscipline and the megabuck', *Accountancy*, March: 67–71.

Davis, E., Hanlon, G. and Kay, J. (1993) 'What internationalisation in services means – The case of accountancy in the UK and Ireland' in H. Cox, J. Clegg and G. Ietto-Gillies, (eds) *The Growth of Global Business: New Strategies*, London: Routledge.

Farmar, T. (1988) *A History of Craig Gardner and Co. – The First Hundred Years*, Dublin: Gill and Macmillan.

Flood, J. (1991) 'Doing business – The management of uncertainty in lawyers' work', *Law and Society Review*, 25(1): 41–72.

Gershuny, J. and Miles, I. (1983) *The New Service Economy*, London: Frances Pinter.

Goode, W.J. (1957) 'Community within a community – The professions', *American Sociological Review*, 22(2): 194–200.

Goreily, T. (1994) 'Rushcliffe fifty years on – The changing role of civil legal aid within the Welfare State', *Journal of Law and Society*, 21(4): 545–66.

Hanlon, G. (1994) *The Commercialisation of Accountancy – Flexible Accumulation and the Transformation of the Service Class*, Basingstoke: Macmillan.

Hanlon, G. (1996a) 'Re-regulation, professionalism and commercisalisation', *Teoria Sociologica 6*.

Hanlon, G. (1996b) 'Casino capitalism and the rise of the "commercialised" service class – An examination of the accountant', *Critical Perspectives on Accounting*, 7: 339–63.

Harrison, B. and Bluestone, B. (1988) *The Great U-Turn – Corporate Restructuring and the Polarising of America*, New York: Basic Books.

Harvey, D. (1989) *The Condition of Postmodernity*, Oxford: Basil Blackwell.

Hughes, E.C. (1963) 'Professions', *Daedalus*, 92(4): 655–68.

Humphrey, C., Mozier, P. and Turley, S. (1992) 'The audit expectations gap – *Plus ça change, plus c'est la même chose?*' *Critical Perspectives on Accounting*, 3: 137–61.

HMSO (1971) *British Labour Statistics – Historical Abstracts 1886–1968, Department of Employment*, London: HMSO.

Jones, E. (1981) *Accountancy and the British Economy 1840–1980 – The Evolution of Ernst and Whinney*, London: Batsford.

Leyshon, A., Daniels, P.W. and Thrift, N. (1987) 'Internationalisation of professional producer services – The case of large accountancy firms', *Working Papers on Producer Services 3*, University of Bristol and The Service Industries Research Centre, Portsmouth Polytechnic.

London Economics Ltd. (1994) *The Competitive Advantage of Law and Accountancy in the City of London*, London: Corporation of London.

Macmillan, L. (1995) *Client Care – A Report of a Survey on the Client Care Provided by the Solicitors in Scotland*, Glasgow: Scottish Consumer Council.

McNair, C.J. (1991) 'Proper compromises – The management control dilemma in public accounting and its impact on auditor independence', *Accounting, Organisations and Society*, 16(7): 635–53.

McNeil, I. (1992) 'Auditors lead way to accountability', *The Observer*, 5 March.

McNulty, T., Whittington, R. and Whipp, R. (1993) 'Practices and market driven change – The experiences of engineers and scientists in industrial research and development laboratories and doctors in NHS hospitals', paper presented at Conference: *Professions and Management*, School of Management, University of Stirling, August.

Marshall, T.H. (1939) 'The recent history of professionalism in relation to social structure and social policy', *Canadian Journal of Economics and Political Science*, 5: 325–40.

Murray, F. (1988) 'The decentralisation of production – The decline of the mass productive worker' in R.E. Pahl (ed.) *On Work – Historical, Comparative and Theoretical Approaches*, Oxford: Basil Blackwell, 258–78.

National Economic Research Associates (NERA) (1992) *Competition in European Accounting*, Dublin: Lafferty Publications.

Perkin, H. (1989) *The Rise of Professional Society*, London: Routledge.

Porter, M. (1990) 'Professional-client relationships and women's reproductive health care' in S. Cunningham-Burley and N. McKeganey (eds) *Readings in Medical Sociology*, London: Tavistock/Routledge: 182–210.

Rajan, A. (1987) *The Second Industrial Revolution?* London: Butterworths.

Sassen, S. (1991) *The Global City – New York, London, Tokyo*, Princeton: Princeton University Press.

Savage, M., Barlow, J., Dickens, P. and Fielding, T. (1992) *Property, Bureaucracy and Culture*, London: Routledge.

Sorensen, J.E., Rhode, J.G. and Lawler III, E.E. (1973) 'The generation gap in public accounting', *Journal of Accountancy*, December: 42–50.

Walby, S. (1993) 'Restructuring health professions – A case of post-Fordism', paper presented to the British Sociological Association, Essex University, April.

Wilensky, H. (1964) 'Professionalisation of everyone', *American Journal of Sociology*, LXX(2): 137–58.

9

PROFESSIONALISM AND POLITICS

Towards a new mentality?

David Marquand

INTRODUCTION

As this book goes to press, little remains of the confident and decisive Conservative regime of the 1980s. Of course, it does not follow that the Conservative Party is bound to lose the 1997 election. Still less does it follow that the New Right paradigm of the 1980s and early 1990s is about to be replaced by a successor. The post-war Labour Government was in comparable disarray for its last eighteen months, and lost the subsequent General Election, but the Keynesian social democratic paradigm which had guided it held the field for another quarter of a century. By the same token, no one who watches Labour's current embarrassment over taxation and public expenditure can doubt that, on certain matters at least, New Right approaches still enjoy at least a vestigial hegemony.

Yet intimations of a possible new paradigm are not difficult to detect – and on the political right as well as on the left. State planning has been discredited, and no one wants to return to it. Keynesian economic management has not been discredited exactly, but changes in the global economy appear to have made it unfeasible, at any rate on the level of the medium-sized nation state. Yet there is a widespread sense that the New Right alternative has now run into the sands – a sense shared even by some of its former supporters. Partly because of this, and partly because of the end of the cold war, the old battle-cries of state against market and socialism against capitalism no longer resonate. Meanwhile, persistent divergencies in the fortunes of market economies have focused attention on the varieties of capitalism, and on their moral and cultural dimensions (Albert, 1991). Endemic unemployment in Europe, the rise of the working poor in the United States, the transformation of labour markets everywhere and the associated threat of fragmentation and anomie have fostered a new concern with the dangers of social exclusion and the prerequisites of social cohesion.

Only time can tell if these intimations will 'gell' into a new governing philosophy, capable of guiding decision makers through the unforeseeable contingencies of political life. Yet it is already possible to detect the emergence of a new political discourse, structured by words like 'stability', 'obligation', 'trust' and 'community', and even of a new political mentality. Left and right alike are groping for a new balance between the individual and the collective, between flexibility and commitment, between institutional constraints and personal autonomy. On the right there is talk of a new, 'civic conservatism'; on the left, of a 'stakeholder economy' (Willetts, 1994; Hutton, 1995). Partly because the professions play crucial roles in all knowledge-intensive societies, and partly because professional values are closely related to the concerns of the new mentality, it seems bound to have far-reaching implications for the relationship between professionalism and politics. It is on these implications that the rest of this chapter will focus.

PROFESSIONALISM AND THE NEW MENTALITY

In principle, the new mentality bodes well for professionals. One of the central themes of this book is the inevitable tension – perhaps even conflict – between the version of economic liberalism espoused by the contemporary New Right and the values and structures of professional life. In New Rightist eyes, the professions are, in essence, market distorting cabals of rent seekers, engaged in an elaborate conspiracy to force the price of their services above their true market value. Professional qualifications close off entry and inhibit competition. The professional ethic, which professionals pray in aid when they are unmasked, is designed to justify and perpetuate these nefarious practices. By virtue of all this, moreover, the professions – or at any rate some professions – are the carriers of an anti-market ideology which must be rooted out if a properly functioning market order is once again to come into being. Doctors, teachers, judges, academics, broadcasters, social workers, civil servants, even barristers and policemen have all felt the lash of the New Right governments of the last eighteen years, not just because their practices conflict with the precepts of economic liberalism, but because those practices embody and transmit an implicit public philosophy subversive of the assumptions on which economic-liberal precepts are based.

Logically, then, the emergence of a mentality less sympathetic to New Right economic liberalism should generate a more profession-friendly climate. The fact that one of the main preoccupations of the new mentality is the need to foster the kind of trust relationships that professional practice has always depended on makes such expectations even more plausible. Yet it would be premature to jump to the conclusion that the relationship between politics and the professions is about to be transformed to the advantage of the latter. New Right ideology is only one of the factors responsible for the profession-unfriendly climate of the recent past; and it is not necessarily the most important factor.

Here, Harold Perkin's now classic studies of the development of industrial society from the 1780s to the 1880s and of the rise of what he called 'professional society' from the 1880s to the 1980s, are particularly helpful (Perkin, 1972 and 1989). In the first of them, he told the story of the struggle between the three 'social ideals' of industrial revolution Britain – the 'aristocratic ideal' of the landed class, the 'entrepreneurial ideal' of the manufacturing middle class and the 'working-class ideal' of the small but growing industrial proletariat. According to Perkin the central theme of early nineteenth-century English history may be found in the victory of the entrepreneurial ideal over the other two. By the middle of the century its triumph was complete. In that very moment, however, the seeds of its downfall were already being sown. For within the entrepreneurial camp there had always been a tension between the interests of the capitalist owner-managers on the one hand and those of the also rising professions, the 'forgotten middle class', on the other. Paradoxically, the victory of the entrepreneurial ideal made it possible for the professions to break away from the entrepreneurial camp. This they did, in the name of an alternative 'professional ideal', which held that 'trained and qualified expertise rather than property, capital or labour should be the chief determinant of status and power in society' (Perkin, 1972: 258).

Perkin's second study told the story of the triumph and subsequent misadventures of this professional ideal. It triumphed in the early twentieth century much as the entrepreneurial ideal had triumphed in the early nineteenth. The result was a 'professional society' in which – despite the continued existence of social classes and continuing recourse to the rhetoric of class struggle – the 'horizontal' divisions between these classes became steadily less significant than the 'vertical' divisions between professional groups. But just as the entrepreneurial ideal had started to decline in the very moment of its triumph, so the professional ideal began to lose its glitter just when it had achieved moral hegemony. As society became more professionalised, with an ever increasing number of professional groups, the groups concerned found themselves engaged in a kind of auction, in which they had to bid against each other for their share of society's resources. Group after group discovered reasons why it was essential for the taxpayer to finance public services to meet the social needs which that same group had identified. The welfare state became ever more hungry for resources as an ever larger number of professional groups sought to expand its boundaries. As the economic climate grew colder and resources become scarcer, the professional camp began to bifurcate, much as the entrepreneurial camp had bifurcated in the nineteenth century. Professionals employed in the private sector came to see the profession-induced growth of the public sector as a threat to their interests; little by little, they began to desert the professional ideal in the name of which that growth had taken place. And, by an extraordinary paradox of historical regression, they did so under the banner of a new version of the entrepreneurial ideal of the early nineteenth century.

This, Perkin argued, is the real meaning of the rise of the New Right. New Rightists proclaim their adherence to the entrepreneurial ideal of the early nineteenth century, and announce their intention to reconstruct society in accordance with the values of free-market liberalism. Their opponents in the left and centre assume that this announcement means what it says. But, in reality, New Right ideology is a camouflage for a social interest which is poles apart from that of the early nineteenth-century owner-manager whose claims were justified by the entrepreneurial ideal in its original form. The owner-manager of the industrial revolution risked his own capital, hired his own labour, invested his own substance and took his own decisions; the entrepreneurial ideal of that era spoke to the social realities of the age. None of this is true of today's private-sector professionals. They are not capital-risking individualists. They are salaried employees, skilled in the service and management of large, bureaucratically organised hierarchies that dominate markets quite unlike the atomistic, competitive markets of 150 years ago. The market-liberal ideology of the New Right appeals to them, not because they really want to put the clock back to the early nineteenth century, a feat which would in any case be beyond them, but because market liberalism is the best available ideological armoury from which to draw the weapons they need to defeat their *frères semblables* in the public sector.

Perkin should not be swallowed whole. Like many pioneers, he rides his horse too hard and too far. His definitions are often imprecise and, worse still, fluctuating. That said, his two studies provide an invaluable prism through which to examine the issues I have been discussing. The most obvious implication is that the New Right's attacks on professionalism and the professional ethic are sectoral rather than ideological in origin. If Perkin is right, the private-sector professionals who have spearheaded the late twentieth-century backlash against professionalism are not motivated by economic doctrine. The reason they wish to clip the wings of the public-sector professionals is not that they genuinely believe that professional structures and practices inhibit the free flow of market forces: their own structures and practices do so too. It is that they and their public-sector counterparts are competing for scarce resources. And, to the extent that that is true, the new mentality I have been discussing will make no difference. Public- and private-sector professionals will still be competing with each other; and the latter will still want to clip the wings of the former.

That is only the beginning of the story. According to Perkin the anti-professional backlash of our time is due, above all, to the 'arrogance' of the professionals. There is something in this, no doubt, but I do not believe that it is anything like the whole story. Two other factors seem to me much more important. One is that professional society is, by definition, knowledge-intensive society; and that the more knowledge-intensive society becomes, the less deferential it will be. A better educated public will be more confident of its own judgement, and less content to take authority on trust. In this perspective, Perkin's backlash against professionalism becomes part of a much wider backlash against traditional authority as such. The growth of alternative medicine; exposures of police malpractice; attacks on allegedly sexist judges; research selectivity exercises in Higher Education; exposures of the private lives of the famous; the customer-provider split in the Health Service; attempts to privatise civil service recruitment; probing television interviews and even the campaign for a written constitution are all part of the 'new populism' which Samuel Beer described ten years ago (Beer, 1982).

The second factor has to do with Fred Hirsch's notion that, as society becomes richer, demand increasingly shifts to positional goods (Hirsch, 1979). The result, as he described it, was a paradox. A positional good is valuable only insofar as it is exclusive to its possessor. Characteristic examples are empty moorlands, quiet lanes, lonely Mediterranean islands. In a wealthy society, more and more people want such goods, but in acquiring them, they destroy them. There is obviously a sense in which professional skills are a classic case of a positional good. Part of the point of acquiring them is to lever oneself up the occupational and status hierarchy. But they provide such a lever because they are scarce. If they become plentiful the lever will not work. Hence the credentialism characteristic of advanced society. Once it was enough to have a school leaving certificate. Then it became necessary to have a degree. Now you need a Master's. Hand in hand with credentialism, however, goes disappointment. New entrants to the professional game painfully acquire professional skills, only to discover that the status they sought still eludes them. Chiropracters have less status than doctors; teachers in the new universities are lower down the pecking order than teachers in the old ones; estate agents rate less highly than barristers. And with disappointment, it is plausible to assume, goes resentment. Professional arrogance may be partly to blame for the backlash against professionalism. Much more significant, I suspect, is the resentment of status-hungry new professionals facing the impervious, path-blocking superiority of the old.

Like the sectoral conflict I discussed a moment ago, these two factors are unlikely to disappear. On the contrary, the very development of professional society is likely to fortify them. The obvious implication is that the professional-unfriendly climate of the recent past is likely to survive the current change of mentality – or, to put it in less dramatic terms, that the professions are likely to remain on the defensive, vulnerable to attack and divided against themselves.

TRUSTING THE PROFESSIONAL ETHIC?

Yet professionalism and the professional ethic are indispensable to the proper functioning of a market economy, at any rate in a complex society of the sort we live in. It is a truism that markets depend upon knowledge. The sovereign consumer enjoys sovereignty only to the extent that she is knowledgeable. If buyers do not know enough to choose among sellers, the market mechanism fails. Now, the trouble with professional services is that only professionals themselves can know whether the service is satisfactory (see chapter 2 for details). If I go to a hairdresser, I know whether my hair was competently cut. If I go to a surgeon, I do not know whether the surgery was competently performed. If I die, it may not be the surgeon's fault; if I am cured, it may not be due to his skill. Only another surgeon can judge the quality of the service. The underlying assumption of the New Right critique of professionalism as a cover for monopolistic rent-seeking is that, if professionals were unable to control entry by keeping out the unqualified, the price of their services would fall to their true market value. But there can be no market unless buyers can trust sellers not to cheat them; and if there were no professional quali-fications to provide a certificate of quality, buyers of professional services could not trust sellers. In these circumstances, the notion of a true market value for professional services – the pivot on which the New Right critique of professionalism turns – confuses more than it illuminates.

One obvious conclusion is that the professional ethic is more than an ideological stalking horse for the interests of the professionals who propagate it. It is also a response to a genuine social need. If professional services are, in some sense, non-marketable, if in this field the competitive market cannot by itself guarantee that the consumer's interests will be properly served, how can the consumer be protected from predatory and unscrupulous producers? With all its obvious imperfections, the profes-sional ethic does at least attempt to answer that question. In effect, it offers society a bargain. Professionals are allowed to rig the market by control-ling entry and regulating supply. In return, they internalise a set of values which prevent them from abusing their market power. They refrain from exploiting their clients, not because they are afraid of competition from other professionals, but because they believe it to be wrong to do so. Market economics cannot make sense of a bargain of that sort, because the postulates of market economics rule out the kind of behaviour it necessit-ates. But that is scarcely a reason for dismissing it as impossible. And once its possibility is conceded, the professional ethic acquires a new meaning. It has to be seen, at least in part, as a mechanism through which society slowly learned to protect itself against the consequences of applying market economics in areas to which they are unsuited.

All this points to a paradox, perhaps even to a contradiction, at the heart of professional society. Such a society is peculiarly dependent on trust. The surgeon's skill, the scholar's learning, the judge's impartiality, the policeman's probity, the social worker's insight have to be taken on trust by those who consume the services they provide. Appraisal systems, league tables, performance indicators, customers' charters and the rest can provide safeguards against the abuse of trust, but they operate in general terms and after the event. At the crucial moment – discussing the pros and cons of an operation with a consultant; instructing a solicitor about a divorce settlement; telling a policeman about the circumstances of a break-in; listening to a tutor's comments on an essay – they pale into insignificance. At such moments, the client has no option but to trust the professional; to withdraw trust is to corrode the essential professional relationship and to degrade the service which it is the professional's duty to provide.

So far, perhaps, so obvious (except, unfortunately, to New Right economic liberals). But at least three implications are much less obvious. One is that, by the same token, professional society depends upon authority. For trust and authority go hand in hand. I trust a professional because, and insofar as, I accept the authority of the professional's office and the authority of those who certified her as competent to exercise her professional functions. The second implication is that, for that very reason, professional society is now in danger of undermining its own foundations. As I tried to argue a moment ago, Samuel Beer's 'new populism' is the bastard child of professionalism; and the 'new populism' is subversive of all forms of authority, including professional authority. Professionals are, by definition, elitists; we pay them because, in their own field, they know more than we do and we therefore defer to them. But populism, whether new or old, is intrinsically anti-elitist; it is at best uneasy with, and at worst downright hostile to, any claim to superiority and to the deference earned by superiority. For populists, the untutored wisdom of the masses counts for more than any painfully-aquired skill. And, in modern mass democracies, all politicians, irrespective of ideology, are tempted (perhaps even obliged) to play to an essentially populist gallery.

That leads on to the third implication. A professional-friendly political climate would have to be, at least to some degree, an elitist climate. It would require the regeneration of trust and therefore the rehabilitation of authority. Despite the tentative emergence of the new mentality I tried to describe at the beginning of this essay, there is not much sign of either in the politics of our time.

146

REFERENCES

Albert, M. (1991) *Capitalisme contre Capitalisme*, Paris: Seuil.

Beer, S.H. (1982) *Britain Against Itself: The political contradictions of collectivism*, London: Faber & Faber.

Hutton, W. (1995) *The State We're In*, London: Jonathan Cape.

Hirsch, F. (1979) *The Social Limits to Growth*, Cambridge: Harvard University Press.

Perkin, H. (1972) *The Origins of Modern English Society 1780–1880*, London: Routledge & Kegan Paul.

Perkin, H. (1989) *The Rise of Professional Society, England Since 1880*, London: Routledge.

Willetts, D. (1991) *Civic Conservatism*, London: Social Market Foundation.

INDEX

Lightning Source UK Ltd.
Milton Keynes UK
UKHW022021101020
371215UK00011B/239